GW00400423

Understanding Borderline Personality Disorder

Discover the Different Types of BPD; Effective Skills to Manage Your Daily Battles and Strategies to Help Others Improve Their Relationship with You

Jennifer C. Dove

FREE BONUSES

Are You Interested in a Couple of <u>FREE BONUSES</u>?

<u>Bonus #1</u> is the TYPES of BPD Quiz. Please note that this quiz is for insight and understanding purposes, <u>not a diagnostic tool</u>.

<u>Bonus #2</u> is an exercise that helps you map out your BPD symptoms alongside their triggers, offering a visual representation of your emotional behaviors.

Click **<u>HERE</u>** or SCAN the Code below to get your ***FREE PDF copy Now***!

Scan me

Contents

Introduction

"Turn your demons into art, your shadow into a friend, your fear into fuel, your failures into teachers, your weaknesses into reasons to keep fighting. Don't waste your pain. Recycle your heart." – Andrea Balt

Your life may feel like a minefield at times. There are bombs and booby traps everywhere. To avoid suffering, you must be very careful where you step. There seems no way to successfully navigate without ending up shell-shocked and metaphorically blown to pieces unless you possess a worldview map. Having borderline personality disorder (BPD) requires a specific type of map.

You can think of mines as intense emotions or thoughts; Once you step on them, everything explodes. Perhaps they are not even your thoughts or feelings but those of someone close to you. Each decision you make can lead to you stepping on a mine that will blow everything apart; however, standing on the spot will not solve the problem. Your reality will not change if you remain precisely where you are. To improve your life, you must get that map and learn how to navigate the minefield.

If you have been diagnosed with BPD or if you know someone who has, you may have questions about the condition and how to deal with it. It can be overwhelming and scary to be diagnosed with borderline personality disorder, but there is information to help you live comfortably. You can try to understand the condition, learn how to manage your emotions effectively, discover proper treatments, and implement strategies to improve relationships. Chapter by chapter, this book will educate you to help you live a better life with BPD. And there are a couple of chapters dedicated to those who live with or are in a relationship with someone with BPD to help them as well have a better life.

There are many questions surrounding this condition, such as what it means, what you should do, or how it will affect your life. After being appropriately assessed, you may be able to understand many of the things you typically experience. However, the feeling that something is wrong can still persist. Most people have a negative view of BPD, so you may feel "strange" and "off" when you finally understand what is happening. No one likes feeling they are different in some way or that they do not quite fit in. But BPD is more common than most people realize, although people tend to underestimate its prevalence.

Despite being less known than other disorders, BPD is more common than illnesses like schizophrenia. In fact, borderline personality disorder affects 1.6% of the population in the United States, according to recent research. This means that over four million people have BPD in America alone.

You have seen characters represent this condition in movies and books (even though you might not be aware of it). For example, the film *Eternal Sunshine of the Spotless Mind* beautifully portrays the chaos, heartbreak, and passion of the relationship between Joel and Clementine, each showing different types of BPD. As each character has traits the other wants, their attraction is inevitable. It is a beautiful demonstration of what happens when you mix these two types of borderline personality disorders.

Joel and Clementine are highly sensitive, but Joel experiences this emotion with an introverted tendency, whereas Clementine is highly extroverted. Depending on their temperaments, each has a different coping style. Unlike Joel, who uses the "flight" threat response to deal with his suffering, Clementine usually "fights." It is apparent from their thoughts and actions that the condition they endure negatively impacts their everyday lives. Can you relate to this?

If you experience borderline personality disorder, you may feel frustrated about the unpredictability of your emotions. It can be difficult for you and those around you to understand and handle your feelings. Emotions that can last for hours or even days and change rapidly make it hard to predict your mood. You may sometimes feel helpless, especially when your feelings are out of control.

Consequently, you may struggle in different areas of your life and feel self-conscious because you feel different. Or you may refrain from reaching out and connecting with people because you cannot imagine how they would want to spend some time with you.

BPD's rollercoaster of emotions triggers several problematic behaviors to cope with suffering; these behaviors seldom succeed. For example, you may numb yourself with drugs or alcohol to "fit in." Frustration, loneliness, and more problems typically follow.

Aside from dealing with your own psychological problems, you probably experience something even more painful: deep misunderstandings from those around you. You might even feel ashamed about your diagnosis. Borderline personality disorder is incredibly stigmatized; people often misunderstand it, which is why someone with BPD will rarely talk about their condition. Their loved ones may also avoid the topic. Because of this, people with BPD often suffer alone in silence, which does not help their situation.

One of the reasons for compiling the information for this book is to challenge common misconceptions. No one should feel misunderstood or alone when it comes to BPD. It is common for those with BPD to receive unnecessary comments due to a lack of understanding of their condition. For instance, being told to "just snap out of it" or to "stop being so dramatic." Perhaps you are beginning to understand that this disorder is not something to simply live with, hoping for the best. You have the right to expect to improve and this isn't a simple task since the information about BPD is often confusing, disjointed, and inconsistent.

Dealing with mental health struggles is not easy. You probably can relate to feelings of helplessness and exhaustion. You can live a fulfilling life and find peace with the correct information. A diagnosis of borderline personality disorder does not mean you must give up on living a meaningful life.

This book is a single, comprehensive resource that will help you navigate through BPD. The goal is to help you understand the complex nature of BPD through research-based information. As you read the following chapters, you will learn the different types of BPD, which will help you address the symptoms effectively. You will discover some common triggers for borderline personality disorder, how to identify them, and strategies to prevent them. Finally, you will also learn what kinds of treatments have been proven to alleviate symptoms of BPD. Using this information, you can better identify the best ways to manage your condition.

Throughout the chapters, you will uncover different aspects of BPD and how they may affect your life (such as relationships and work). The book will cover the struggles, coping strategies, and emotions associated with this condition. You will learn how to get the help you need and maximize that help by taking care of your body and mind with daily habits.

Families, partners, and friends of those with BPD can often feel powerless or overwhelmed in their attempts to help them. This book will give you a better understanding of what it is like to live with this disorder. Through new insights, you will gain knowledge of the condition, allowing you to better care for and support someone who suffers from BPD. In addition, this book offers concrete steps for those who interact with someone with borderline personality disorder. With this knowledge, you will be giving them the opportunity to cope with this condition in a way that improves and changes their lives for the better, as well as yours.

Considering that BPD is associated with poor interpersonal relationships, it is not surprising that people around BPD sufferers are also greatly affected by its effects. Having a relative with this disorder can be stressful. Caregivers or family members may unintentionally act in ways that can worsen their loved one's symptoms. Since they are unsure how to respond to or handle their loved ones during this time, family members usually have difficulty helping them. In dealing with someone with this condition, you may not know what to say or how to say it; that is why some people describe living with someone with BPD as walking on eggshells. Therefore, a section of this practical guide is dedicated to how family members, friends, partners, and co-workers can support those with borderline personality disorder. As you read on, you will find answers to your questions and concerns regarding this disorder. You will also learn what to expect and how you can best support a person suffering from BPD. It offers strategies on what to say or not say and what to do or not do to avoid making situations worse. And in doing so, it will make everyone's life better.

BPD has always been a misunderstood illness. Those who suffer from this illness often feel alone and do not know how to ask for help; however, they need comfort, encouragement, and reassurance that people are willing to listen to them.

Borderline personality disorder is a diagnosis that does not come with a quick fix. The challenge for those suffering from BPD and their loved ones is to realize that there are different ways of approaching the illness. This book aims to educate both groups (BDP sufferers and those who interact with them) about BPD's diverse perspectives and aspects.

Although borderline personality disorder can change someone's life, many can still find meaning and purpose. This book aims to accomplish two things. First, to enable those with BPD to feel more in control of their condition and to be better equipped to manage their emotions, relationships, and other aspects of their life. And second, for those closest to BPD sufferers, to offer viable strategies to interact with the sufferer to support them and improve their life. Whether you struggle with BPD or you have a loved one who does, this book can provide you with answers to questions you might have. Please keep reading to find research-based information that will help you and those closest to you better understand borderline personality disorder and how to manage it and live a better life.

Chapter One

A Closer Look at Borderline Personality Disorder (BPD)

The world stopped for a moment in 2022 when a psychiatrist publicly diagnosed Amber Heard with "Borderline Personality Disorder" during her defamation trial with Johnny Depp. For some, it was the first time hearing these three words; for others, it was a diagnosis they have had all their lives. BPD has become the interest of the general public worldwide.

Much was learned about Borderline Personality Disorder because of the Depp-Heard trial. Since Heard was already perceived negatively, the most common fear was that BPD would be linked to her behavior (drugs, rage, abuse, violence), mainly because it was an already stigmatized and misunderstood condition.

When the psychiatrist testified in the defamation trial that Amber Heard suffered from various mental disorders, BDP became linked to her outrageous behavior; borderline personality disorder is more than just rage, violence, and aggression. People with BPD and experts worldwide disapproved of using the BPD label to discredit Heard.

Many people with this diagnosis suffer quietly, even as others express their suffering by lashing out. BPD is a stigmatized disease because it is not discussed often in mainstream media, except in extreme cases of abuse or violence.

The sudden publicity over this mental health condition made many stand up to share a clear and powerful truth with the world: people with BPD are not "broken." These individuals have what Dr. Marsha Linehan[1] calls a "skills deficit." Their emotions are intense, and they have not learned the skills to feel, process, and manage their lives.

Why is BPD so Misunderstood?

Borderline personality disorder patients face two types of problems: those caused directly by the disorder and those caused by discrimination. Discrimination-related issues tend to be more persistent and hard to overcome. One of the biggest obstacles in the recovery process for patients with BPD is constantly being judged and misinterpreted as:

- Dangerous to themselves and others

- Manipulative

- Attention-seeking

- Difficult to work with

- Resistant to treatment

These negative characteristics reduce our understanding of people with this condition to just their symptoms. A person with BPD does not lack identity, desire, or willpower. They struggle with emotions and compensate for this lack of skills by performing behaviors that aren't always beneficial for themselves and others. They generally feel isolated, misunderstood, and suffer greatly; however, their lack of skills should not prevent them from reaching their true potential.

In reality, stigmatizing attitudes exist to a greater extent than we realize. Many healthcare providers continue to label people with BPD as "manipulative," "attention-seeking," and "dangerous." BPD patients tend to generate negative countertransference in health professionals, creating a misunderstanding of their condition.

Understandably, some mental health clinicians may put emotional distance from patients with BPD to protect themselves from the distressing types of behaviors. This might be especially problematic for patients with BPD since they're more sensitive to rejection and abandonment. As a result, when clinicians distance themselves from patients in mental health care, they may unintentionally encourage those patients to engage in unhealthy behaviors to cope with the perceived threat.

For this reason, some professionals limit the number of BPD patients they are willing to see or refuse to treat people with BPD. For a therapist who is not adequately trained in treating BPD, sessions may be frustrating and uncomfortable for all parties involved. Providers may feel inadequate and ineffective.

Defining Borderline Personality Disorder

People tend to minimize different mental conditions, such as BPD, to a collection of symptoms. The idea that people with BPD are "aggressive, impulsive, and unstable" diminishes the validity of this health condition.

The Diagnostic and Statistical Manual of Mental Disorders (DSM-5) model identifies BPD as a cluster B personality disorder, which includes antisocial, borderline, histrionic, and narcissistic classifications. This cluster comprises conditions that affect a person's emotional functioning, leading to behaviors others may see as extreme or irrational. As BPD involves challenges on different levels (interpersonal, self-image, emotions, and behaviors), it is a complex mental health condition.

When someone has BPD, they feel emotions intensely and for a long time. Returning to a baseline emotional level becomes extremely challenging after an emotional event. This loss of dynamic control can affect how a person feels, increase impulsivity, and negatively impact their relationships with others.

BPD patients struggle with identifying and understanding their emotions, making them feel unsafe and unloved. Two effects may result from this:

- They usually develop an intense fear of abandonment or instability and have difficulty being alone.

- They may show inappropriate anger and impulsiveness, resulting in wild mood swings. Individuals may push others away, even though they want to build good relationships.

Understanding BPD starts by comprehending that it's a disorder that affects how you think and feel about yourself and others, making it hard to function in everyday life.

Risk Factors and Causes

Globally, different theories affirm that BPD results from biological factors, invalidating environments, and early trauma (such as child abuse). Invalidating settings are those in which emotional management is not encouraged by caregivers.

Although most children struggle to control their actions when strong emotions appear, some may have a challenging time regulating how to manage their feelings. This is due to specific biological vulnerabilities (genetic, temperamental). If children with these vulnerabilities are immersed in invalidating environments, they can develop emotional dysregulation (a primary symptom of BPD) with time.

BPD is associated with the following biological vulnerabilities:

Genetics

Genetics are believed to be responsible for borderline personality disorder. A family history of BPD increases your risk of developing the condition.

Brain Differences

Behavior and emotional parts of the brain don't communicate properly in people who suffer from BPD. Their brains work differently because of these problems.

Emotional Vulnerabilities

Studies have shown that babies are born with temperaments regarding how they manage emotions. Children with special emotional needs make a lot of demands on their parents and they may be unfairly blamed for how their struggles affect the family.

BPD is linked to the following environmental factors:

Invalidation

There is a significant risk of developing BPD when a child's communication of private emotional experiences is ignored, punished, or minimized. An invalidating family situation can damage a person's self-esteem as it is being developed in childhood.

A dysfunctional family environment interacting with a child's innate temperament or genetics can lead to BPD. The chances increase further if an invalidating environment or genetic risk factors are combined with childhood trauma (sexual assault, bullying, or other childhood stressors).

Childhood Abuse and Trauma

Approximately 70% of those with BPD have experienced sexual, emotional, or physical abuse as children. BPD is also associated with parental substance use disorder, separation from the mother, and poor maternal attachment.

Symptoms

Feeling vulnerable or having mood changes are everyday human experiences.

When an individual is given a diagnosis of BPD based on the Diagnostic and Statistical Manual of Mental Disorders (DSM-5), it is determined that many of the symptoms listed below are severe in degree and long-lasting.

According to the manual, BPD is defined as follows:

Borderline Personality Disorder (DSM-5 301.83 - F60. 3)[2]

BPD is a pervasive pattern of instability in interpersonal relationships, self-image, and emotion, as well as marked impulsivity beginning by early adulthood and present in a variety of contexts, as indicated by five (or more) of the following:

- Chronic feelings of emptiness

- Emotional instability in reaction to day-to-day events (e.g., intense episodic sadness, irritability, or anxiety usually lasting a few hours and only rarely more than a few days)

- Frantic efforts to avoid real or imagined abandonment

- Identity disturbance with markedly or persistently unstable self-image or sense of self

- Impulsive behavior in at least two areas that are potentially self-damaging (e.g., spending, sex, substance abuse, reckless driving, binge eating)

- Inappropriate, intense anger, or difficulty controlling anger (e.g., frequent displays of temper, constant anger, recurrent physical fights)

- A pattern of unstable and intense interpersonal relationships characterized by extremes between idealization and devaluation (also known as "splitting")

- Recurrent self-harming, suicidal behavior, gestures, or threats

- Transient, stress-related paranoid ideation or severe dissociative symptoms

People with BPD experience different symptoms which can vary in severity, frequency, and duration.

Also, people with borderline personality disorder are commonly terrified of abandonment, whether real or imagined. They respond to this fear and show frantic efforts to avoid such abandonment. Even patients who are expecting separation may experience intense fears of abandonment. For example, a common situation is BPD patients panicking or becoming angry when they cannot see their therapist, even if the therapist previously informed them that they were going to be away on vacation.

Intense and frequent relationship changes are a hallmark of BPD. There is a tendency among patients to love their partners, relatives, and other people deeply. Changing values, interests, or goals dramatically can alter that love quickly. Identity problems, such as a weak perception of self and abandonment fears, are also a big part of BPD which may contribute to self-harm behaviors. One such significant BPD symptom is impulsivity.

An impulsive person may abuse drugs, drive recklessly, gamble, overeat, have unsafe sex, or spend too much money. BPD patients often feel an overwhelming sense of emptiness. Self-harm behaviors such as cutting, picking, and burning are common ways to cope with negative feelings, as are suicidal thoughts, threats, and behaviors.

As said before, BPD is characterized by difficulty controlling emotions. Anger may be disproportionate or inappropriate, according to the DSM-5. As a result, temper problems or physical fights can occur.

The key to creating a meaningful and honest relationship with someone with BPD lies in understanding the behavior. Despite an individual's seemingly erratic and disturbing behavior, a lot is happening behind the scenes.

BPD by Age

BPD may develop in stages:

- Childhood: premorbid stage

- Adolescence: subclinical age

- Late adolescence: first full BPD episode

- Adulthood: remission and relapse

Despite childhood being a critical stage of BPD development, symptoms can first be identified during adolescence. Most adults with BPD report self-harming before age 13, while 30% say they began this behavior between the ages of 13 and 17.

In typical adolescents, impulsivity, identity issues, and affective instability diminish as they age. In the case of those with BPD, these symptoms tend to worsen over time.

When people with BPD reach adulthood, they may switch from impulsivity and suicidal to negative interpersonal behavior. There is a decrease in BPD diagnoses from young to middle adulthood; however, relapses are common.

Despite these most common stages, not everyone with BPD goes through each.

About Fear and Awareness

In 2009, Time Magazine published an article titled "Borderline Personality: The Disorder Doctors Fear Most." In the 14 years since then, little has changed; people worldwide still misunderstand BPD. Those with this disorder also carry an intense stigma and deep shame. In some cases, being identified as someone who suffers from BPD means being despised or even feared.

It is human nature to fear the unknown. As a society, people need to realize there is nothing to fear. Real change can happen when people understand what BPD truly is.

The public spotlight may help raise awareness of borderline personality disorder; however, it can also result in an entirely negative outcome. By stigmatizing the condition, those with BPD are less likely to seek help, which can worsen symptoms.

It is the same for people with BPD as it is for everyone else. They excel at some things and struggle with others. With some help, these individuals can create a life they can be proud to live. The following chapters will include more information about the characteristics and complications of BPD.

TAKEAWAYS

According to the DSM-V, BPD is a pervasive pattern of instability in interpersonal relationships, self-image, and emotion and marked impulsivity beginning in early adulthood. BPD can appear in a variety of contexts. It belongs to cluster B personality disorders, divided into four types: antisocial, borderline, histrionic, and narcissistic.

- Several factors can cause BPD:

  - Biological vulnerabilities: genetics, brain differences, and emotional vulnerabilities

  - Environmental factors: abuse, trauma, and invalidation in childhood

- The development of BPD begins in adolescence. Children tend to develop impulsivity, identity issues, and affective instability as they grow up. When they reach adulthood, they may switch from impulsivity and suicidality to negative interpersonal behavior.

- Those who have BPD face two main problems. First, they struggle with emotions, feel isolated, misunderstood, and suffer greatly. They may face discrimination, be viewed as dangerous to themselves and others, manipulative, attention-seeking, and challenging to treat. And second, the general public struggles to understand BPD.

- BPD involves difficulties on different levels: interpersonal, self-image, emotions, and behaviors. People with this condition experience intense emotions and have not learned the skills to process and manage them effectively.

- Effects of BDP:

  - Abandonment fears and difficulty being alone.

  - Inappropriate anger, impulsiveness, mood swings, and pushing others away.

- Symptoms include instability in interpersonal relationships, self-image, emotions, and marked impulsivity. These symptoms are often severe and long-lasting.

Chapter Two
Digging Deeper Into BPD

To better understand BPD, consider the chameleon. The chameleon is one of the most interesting animals on this planet. They have an elongated tongue, independently moving eyes, and an ability to change color depending on the circumstances; this makes them unique among similar species.

Chameleons adapt to the environment when they face a threat. Rather than manipulation, this action is a defense mechanism to cope with difficult situations by blending into the background.

In addition, a chameleon's eyes move in many directions independently; the same goes for the emotions, thoughts, and behaviors of people with BPD. They act, feel, and think unexpectedly and generally contradict their own intentions.

People who are hurting and have little hope need to hold onto other people's energy. The powerful tongue of chameleons enables them to latch on to what they need (for example, food), like the need for BDP patients to hold on to others. Due to their lack of self-confidence, people with BPD usually believe outside proposals may solve their problems. When that doesn't happen, they move slowly, feeling hopeless, apathetic, and empty, waiting for someone or something to soothe their pain, fill their void, or compel them to act.

There is a point in which people with BPD and chameleons differ significantly. The defensive mechanisms of those who suffer from BPD are more complex than they seem; a lot goes on beneath the surface.

Types of BPD

According to experts, borderline personality disorder is classified into four categories based on different symptoms that the person may show. These four types are: discouraged, impulsive, petulant, and self-destructive.

Compared to someone with discouraged BDP, who might seem hopeless and self-harm more often, someone with impulsive BPD may live a riskier life.

The various kinds of BPD may present the same symptoms at times, but there are clear indicators to differentiate each variety of the disorder. Although someone with discouraged BPD can be depressed like someone with impulsive BPD, the second kind will show anger and aggression. In contrast, an individual with discouraged BPD is more likely to turn to isolation. Typically, aggression and anger are good markers of the different types (impulsive BPD may be more aggressive than petulant BPD, for instance). A person with petulant BPD usually lingers between anger and not trusting others, and the self-destructive type is prone to self-sabotage. In some individuals, multiple versions of BPD can be present at any given time. In addition, others may not fit into any of the categories.

Here are the four types in detail:

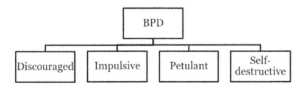

Discouraged Borderline

Those with discouraged borderline symptoms often seem needy and dependent, but their anger towards others and disillusionment are hidden. Those with this profile are anxious to be accepted and approved; however, they may feel inadequate or inferior, leading to potential depression.

They tend to be clingy, follow the crowds, and go around feeling gloomy and somewhat downcast. Deep down, they are often angry and disappointed by the actions of those around them. If untreated, people with discouraged borderline tendencies are more likely to resort to self-harm as a coping mechanism; if they don't get help, they can become suicidal.

WHAT DOES DISCOURAGED BPD LOOK LIKE?
[Mike]

I have always struggled with emotions, weight loss, and social anxiety. My first time in a psychiatric hospital was when I was 16 and admitted with depressive and obsessive-compulsive symptoms.

Deep down, it has been a sensation I've always carried with me. I don't think I know when everything started falling apart or when I started feeling so bad about myself. I always lived in a small town with my family, went to the same school, and did the same activities. Since I can remember, I have loved painting, and my parents always said I had a talent for it.

Around 17, I won a scholarship for a modern art summer course in Italy, but my parents couldn't afford the flight. That summer, my dream was crushed, and my emotions went with it. Attending school was always tough for me, so art was all I had.

I experienced multiple traumatic events, which I would call "emotional bullying." These events caused me to drop out of high school. After that, I gradually became socially withdrawn. The more I retracted from my peers, the more I filled my time with things that turned into addictions, such as watching anime.

As a result, depression and obsessive-compulsive disorder developed. At that point, I was timid, emotionally unstable, sensitive to criticism, a perfectionist, rigid, hesitant, and critical of myself.

When I was 18, my father took me to the emergency room with an extreme episode of severe anxiety and irrational fears. The doctors in the hospital diagnosed me with BPD.

With time and professional help, my life started to change. I started taking medication, along with going to individual and group therapy.

My last psychotherapeutic sessions focused on personal life goals and daily structure. Discussing the plans for each day, easing the burden of tasks (the stress caused by academic papers and exams), and cultivating abilities such as drawing are some areas we addressed.

Impulsive Borderline

Impulsive borderline personality disorder appears to be a close cousin of Histrionic personality disorder. Those with this type of BDP are flirtatious, charming, charismatic, elusive, and superficial. Their energy level is high, and they constantly seek thrills. They seem insatiable in their desire for attention or excitement and are often easily bored. As the name 'impulsive' implies, they frequently act without thinking, getting into all sorts of trouble.

These BPD types like to be noticed but also have strong antisocial instincts; they want to control how they engage with others. Attempting to be the center of attention and avoiding boredom can lead to risky actions. Frequently, people with impulsive BPD act rashly without considering the consequences, and in some cases, these actions result in injuries or developing addictions.

WHAT DOES IMPULSIVE BPD LOOK LIKE?

[Jack]

I was 42 when I was admitted to a psychiatric facility for attempted suicide. Compulsive gambling had been a part of my life for six years. The situation had gotten out of control when I lost all my money.

I was single without children, unemployed, and worked low-skilled jobs. I had been involved in romantic relationships before, but they never lasted long, and many turned violent; I have a restraining order from one of my ex-partners.

I can partly explain my behaviors because I had taken different drugs since my teenage years. I smoked tobacco at 12, drank alcohol at 14, and had occasional social use of cannabis during that time. During my 20s, I smoked one pack of cigarettes a day and started using cocaine. That was the most destructive stage of my life.

At 36, I began gambling, which became my most problematic behavior. Sometimes I felt like I could control it, but I gambled more than I could afford monetarily to escape reality.

Getting into a psychiatric institution after my suicide attempt was the first step toward building a better life for myself.

Petulant Borderline

The petulant borderline subtype description includes the following characteristics:

- Unpredictable

- Irritable

- Impatient

- Complaining

- Defiant

- Upset

- Foolish

- Pessimistic

- Resentful

People with petulant borderline personality disorder have difficulty trusting others. They vacillate between feelings of unworthiness and feelings of anger.

In addition to being easily irritated, they quickly become disillusioned when they don't get what they want and are prone to outbursts of anger and frustration.

The tendency to be willful and defiant results in their being stubborn, defensive, and unwilling to admit their faults. Although they may have loving relationships, their relationships are complex, and they often engage in passive-aggressive behaviors to lash out at people who displease them.

WHAT DOES PETULANT BPD LOOK LIKE?

[Jacob]

At age 20, I sought help for petulant borderline personality disorder, which had made healthy relationships nearly impossible for me. At that time, I had no idea that the illness made everything harder, but getting the appropriate treatment was life-changing.

My childhood was difficult. After being neglected by irresponsible parents who struggled with addictions, social services placed me in a foster home. After being moved four more times to other foster homes, my parents' parental rights were removed, and my foster parents adopted me.

Even though my adoptive parents were kind and wanted me to succeed at school and to make friends, I never felt close to them. Even though I felt comfortable with them, I could never feel close to them, so I started creating this "secret" life behind their backs. Whether the secret was big or small, it didn't matter; I simply enjoyed keeping secrets from my adoptive family.

While I liked my family, I never quite trusted them; I don't remember ever trusting anyone, not even my friends at school, especially as I grew up. What might have been a minor disappointment to someone else, like a friend feeling sick and canceling plans, had always been an unbearable event to me that often resulted in self-harm to numb the pain. Self-harming was also my way of crying out. As I felt alone and didn't trust anyone, getting attention provided me with comfort in the short term.

My friendships never lasted long. I usually envisioned that the new friends I made were flawless, and when they didn't meet my high expectations, I would feel intense frustration or anger and tell my friends, "If you cared about me, you would....".

I sought professional people. This new ability to trust was vital to help me start building genuine relationships and understanding that not everyone will meet my expectations.

Self-Destructive Borderline

Lastly, there is the self-destructive borderline type. These individuals suffer from severe self-loathing, leading to dangerous or unhealthy habits, including poor health care, reckless driving, and humiliating sexual behavior. An inner sense of bitterness is prevalent in this category. It is common for people with this type to engage in self-destructive behaviors, either consciously or unconsciously.

Self-destructive borderline individuals are their own worst enemies, as their name implies. These people tend to sabotage their progress when things seem to be going well.

People who suffer from self-destructive BPD lack a stable sense of self, resulting in a dependence on others; this creates a fear of abandonment, which is a big issue in their lives.

According to experts, we can't assume someone will have symptoms from one subtype alone; BPD's boundaries are too fluid and susceptible to environmental influences to be reduced to a formula.

Typically, people with BPD experience a great deal of emotional pain. Even though everyone experiences BPD differently, those suffering from self-destructive BPD tend to 'split'. Splitting is a common strategy of black-and-white thinking that fails to bring together both the positive and negative qualities of someone.

WHAT DOES SELF-DESTRUCTIVE BPD LOOK LIKE?
[Brenda]

As a child, my parents divorced, leaving me with a mother who suffered from depression. Despite this, I could make friends, excel academically, and play soccer for my high school team.

While everything seemed okay on the outside, I grew up hating myself so profoundly that I rarely believed anyone could feel differently about me; I honestly thought I did not deserve to be loved.

As a teenager, when I said the wrong thing in class, messed up a play in a soccer game, or felt like an outlier among my friends, I had a habit of stealing alcohol from the liquor cabinet before my mom got home to numb the self-hatred.

When I got to college, I started dating Tom. There had never been a time when I felt as good as I did when we were together. There were moments of relief from my self-hate; however, an intense fear arose with that new love experience. I would often think, "How could he love me like he said he did?" With time, I now understand that I idolized Tom; I felt he was the best part of my life.

At the start of Tom's senior year, he informed me he was accepted with a full scholarship to a post-graduate program abroad; my world was crushed. I felt betrayed and had no idea how to go on.

Years of keeping my emotions inside exploded because of Tom leaving. I couldn't handle my feelings and hated myself for thinking someone could love me. After that, I started individual therapy and found my way out of the deep suffering I have always carried inside.

Splitting

This defense mechanism is considered one of the most primitive since it starts right from the birth of the human infant. Babies must distinguish what is pleasant from what is frustrating to organize their cognitive world.

If they do not do so, they will be confused and incapable of defending themselves from danger because they won't know from where it comes.

It is essentially a defensive strategy to distinguish between the good and the bad, the dangerous and the harmless, and the pleasant and unpleasant. As a result, we will always know what to do, where danger lurks, and how to prepare.

Various experts have described splitting as "all or nothing" thinking, a cognitive distortion prevalent in BPD. This way of thinking tends to see reality in terms of mutually exclusive categories, "black or white," rather than a continuum of grey.

A person with BPD may love or hate someone, but it is inconceivable that these feelings could coexist.

Due to splitting, people living with borderline personality disorder cannot perceive that positive and negative qualities can coexist in themselves or others; they only see them as polarized extremes.

In turn, this impacts how they relate to others and how they view themselves. BPD sufferers also exhibit contradictory visions of themselves that alternate from day to day or even hour to hour. A person might feel like the king of the universe in the morning and then the unhappiest and most lonely person in the afternoon.

Often, splitting occurs suddenly and cyclically. It can take days, weeks, months, or even years for a splitting episode to end. In the mind of the BPD sufferer, the split prevents the coexistence of different options since "dividing the world into good and bad makes it easier to understand."

What Triggers Splitting?

The development of splitting mechanisms depends heavily on interpersonal relationships. For example, not receiving what they need from others (mother, father, loved ones) is a long-term trigger for splitting.

In addition, BPD sufferers usually "split" after something that triggers extreme emotional reactions. The events could be relatively ordinary, such as going on a business trip or getting into an argument. If they split after a disagreement with their boss, they may suddenly consider the boss ungrateful and highly unfair.

What Results from Splitting?

Splitting has a detrimental effect on relationships and self-perception in the long run.

Relationships

People with borderline personality disorder who split can switch between intense feelings of love and intense feelings of hatred. Therefore, this defense mechanism can be distressing for everyone in a relationship, including those people around a person with BPD.

Several problems can manifest in relationships because of splitting. The inability to see warning signs of danger in someone they believe to be infallible makes someone with BPD vulnerable to harm. Also, building a codependent relationship with the person they think is 'perfect.' The constant need for reassurance from the "perfect" person exhausts both parties. Finally, slights, big or small, from the "perfect" person that cause the person with BPD to feel unloved, abandoned, or low often lead to the "perfect" person being viewed as evil. For people with BPD, this can lead to anger towards themselves or others, depression, and withdrawal over time.

Self

Those with borderline personality disorder who use splitting to cope with hurt may experience multiple consequences regarding their self-perception.

In other words, the first consequence of splitting is a distorted or poor self-image. This leads to severe and unsafe behaviors such as self-harm, suicidal thoughts or attempts, chronic feelings of emptiness, and unhealthy, impulsive, or dangerous decision-making.

Black-and-white feelings caused by borderline personality disorder splitting can overwhelm the person experiencing them and those around them. You can imagine how difficult it can be for someone to live with this disorder, considering that this is only one of the many symptoms and characteristics. In the long run, BPD symptoms, such as splitting, can become easier to manage and less intrusive with treatment.

WHAT DOES SPLITTING LOOK LIKE?
[Sara]

Despite some minor ups and downs, I generally felt good about myself. One Saturday, I set out on a road trip by myself. At one point, instead of turning right, I made a wrong turn and got temporarily lost. The high self-esteem I felt about the trip suddenly vanished, and I started criticizing myself.

A lot of negative self-talk went on, such as, "I am such an idiot; I always get lost" and "I am so worthless, I cannot do anything right."

Making a wrong turn when driving doesn't mean someone is worthless. I know that. But because of my BPD, I had a distorted perception of myself to avoid the anxiety of others perceiving me as useless, which was my greatest fear.

Complications and Correlations from BPD

Borderline personality disorder can be very damaging in multiple ways. It can negatively affect intimate relationships, work, school, and self-image, resulting in the following:

- Changing jobs or losing jobs repeatedly

- Not completing one's education

- Several legal issues, including jail time

- Relationship conflicts, marital problems, or divorce

- Frequent hospitalizations and self-injury, such as cutting or burning

- Being involved in abusive relationships

- Unplanned pregnancies, sexually transmitted infections, motor vehicle accidents, and physical fights are caused by impulsive and risky behavior.

Correlations

It may seem strange that you are likely to have another personality disorder besides the one you already deal with, but this is very common. People with personality disorders are more likely to suffer from anxiety, mood disorders, impulse control, and substance abuse issues.

According to the National Institute of Mental Health, borderline personality disorder patients who refuse treatment are more likely to develop other medical issues and mental illnesses. It is estimated that about 15 percent of people with BPD also have bipolar disorder, according to studies[3]

The most common related disorders are:

- Depression

- Eating disorders

- Post-traumatic stress disorder (PTSD)

- Gambling addiction

- Social phobia

- Substance use disorders

- Anxiety disorders.

People with borderline personality disorder and those around them can find it challenging to deal with the symptoms of this disorder, regardless of the type. Despite this, it is reassuring to know that proper help is available regarding diagnosis and treatment.

TAKEAWAYS

- People with borderline personality disorder desperately try to adapt to the environment and other people. Their emotions, thoughts, and behaviors change unexpectedly, and they expect someone or something to soothe their pain, fill their void, or compel them to act. If that doesn't happen, they feel hopeless, apathetic, and empty.

- There are four types of borderline personality disorder:

  - Discouraged — This type of BPD hides anger and disappointment towards others by being needy and dependent.

  - Impulsive — An individual with an impulsive borderline personality disorder is characterized by a strong desire for attention and excitement, causing them to be easily bored. They are flirtatious, charming, elusive, and superficial.

  - Petulant — This kind of borderline personality disorder fluctuates between feelings of unworthiness and anger. They are willful, defiant, stubborn, defensive, and unwilling to admit their faults. It is easy for the individual to become irritated, disillusioned, and frustrated, leading to anger and frustration outbursts.

  - Self-destructive — Those with this BPD type have an inner sense of bitterness, which leads them to engage in self-destructive behaviors. The lack of a stable sense of self makes them dependent on others.

- Splitting is an evolutionary defensive strategy to distinguish between the good and the bad. Splitting affects relationships and self-perception in the long run. We can identify borderline personality disorder with the cognitive distortion of "all or nothing" thinking. People with this condition struggle to perceive that positive and negative qualities can coexist in themselves or others.

- Love and hatred can alternate intensely in relationships. As a result, they tend to build codependent relationships and cannot see risks.

- Their poor self-image leads to self-harming behaviors, suicidal thoughts or attempts, and feelings of emptiness.

- People with personality disorders are more likely to suffer from anxiety, mood and eating disorders, impulse control, depression, and substance abuse issues.

Chapter Three
Turning to Professionals

"I made a vow to God that I would get myself out of hell and that, once I did, I would go back into hell and get others out."
-Marsha Linehan

During the 1960s, mental illness was poorly understood among the general public. Due to this limited knowledge, Marsha Linehan (creator of Dialectical Behavior Therapy [DBT]) was one of many people who were misdiagnosed and treated inappropriately.

Problematic behaviors in adolescence overshadowed Martha's "normal" childhood. It was common for Marsha to attack herself, burning her wrists with cigarettes, cutting herself with sharp objects, and slashing her arms, legs, and midsection. Because of these problems, Marsha's parents had no idea what to do with her. Marsha was confined to a mental health institution for two years in March 1961. After being discharged from the hospital in 1963, the doctors noted in her file that she had been "one of the most disturbed patients in the hospital for a considerable part of the time."

She took an incredible path after leaving the mental health institution. In 1971, Marsha earned a doctoral degree in clinical psychology from

Loyola University. She decided to treat people with borderline personality disorder, the very diagnosis she had.

Once a doctor, Marsha chose to work with highly suicidal people in her practice. She chose the worst cases because she knew how unfortunate they were. She created DBT in response to this need.

Dr. Linehan discovered the power of radical acceptance through her own experience. Real change can only be achieved through the complete acceptance of the individual. Acceptance and change are two sides of the same coin; we cannot have one without the other.

Back in her earlier days, Marsha Linehan did not have an answer. Today, there are many approaches you can use to treat BPD, whether it is in its very early or advanced stages.

Can BPD Be Prevented?

Unfortunately, there is no way to prevent borderline personality disorder. Yet, understanding biological tendencies, developing skills to cope with emotional vulnerabilities, and creating a validating environment can reduce the risk of severe BDP.

This is because, as mentioned before, several factors contribute to the development of this condition, including genetics, emotional vulnerabilities, traumatic experiences, and an invalidating environment.

We cannot alter our genetics or brain development because biology is beyond our control. Recognizing signs of borderline personality disorder is essential to getting treatment as soon as possible if you are at an increased risk of developing the condition.

Adolescent borderline personality disorder symptoms are associated with severe academic and work performance deficiencies and significant relational deficits throughout life. Thus, adolescents who have been diagnosed with BPD early would benefit from treatment programs. A person with BPD who receives early detection and treatment can reduce the severity of their symptoms and improve their psychosocial functioning.

It is also possible to work on skills that compensate for emotional vulnerabilities, such as mindfulness or distress tolerance skills. Mindfulness skills teach you to observe and experience reality as it is presently, to be less judgmental, and to live in the moment, effectively. By incorporating distress tolerance skills, you learn to accept yourself and the present situation without judgment.

Finally, if you are a caregiver of someone who might have borderline personality disorder, you can undoubtedly create a validating environment, which can help prevent the condition from fully developing.

Here are some suggestions for creating a more validating environment:

- As much as possible, maintain healthy relationships between family members (especially couples) so that children can grow up without violence or substance abuse problems.

- When there are marital disagreements or when a couple is divorcing or separating, avoid using children as scapegoats or blackmail.

- If you notice outbursts of anger, self-injurious behavior, or suicide attempts, seek professional assistance immediately, as these signs require immediate attention.

- Make sure they value themselves and their opinions, highlighting their uniqueness, avoiding comparisons, and not idealizing others.

- Give your children the opportunity to make mistakes and learn from them while comforting them and listening to their feelings so they can express their frustration healthily.

- If their academic performance is below the class average, be curious about what's going on and provide help immediately so their self-esteem is not negatively impacted.

When Should You Seek Professional Help?

If borderline personality disorder symptoms interfere with a sufferer's quality of life, it is time to seek medical care. Divorce, job loss, or relationship issues are some of the common reasons individuals with BPD seek help.

It is also important to note that other symptoms indicate a need for treatment, including eating disorders, sleep problems, significant depression, anger, anxiety, mood swings, and thoughts of suicide or death.

How Is BPD Diagnosed?

No definitive test, such as a blood test, can determine if an individual has borderline personality disorder. As a result, professionals conduct a mental health interview to determine whether the previously described symptoms exist.

A psychiatrist, psychologist, or clinical social worker can diagnose borderline personality disorder based on the Diagnostic and Statistical Manual of Mental Disorders (DSM-5). Typically, BPD is diagnosed in late adolescence or early adulthood. However, someone younger than 18 may be found to have borderline personality disorder if there are significant symptoms that last at least a year.

To do so, the mental health professional will perform a thorough interview and discuss their findings with consultants. The questions they ask will shed light on the following:

- History of mental illness in the family and personal medical history.

- A history of previous employment, relationships, and daily life.

- The ability to control their impulses.

Mental health professionals often work with their family and friends to gain more insight into a person's behavior and history.

In addition, mental health professionals may investigate whether the individual has thoughts of self-harm, suicide, or other homicidal thoughts.

Mental health practitioners frequently refer clients for physical examinations and any necessary tests to better understand how BPD manifests or to rule out other possible causes of the symptoms.

What Can I Do to Help Someone With BPD?

- Understand what your loved one is going through by learning about BPD.

- Encourage this person to seek treatment for BPD and to ask about family therapy if they are a relative.

- Provide emotional support, understanding, and patience. People with BPD find change difficult and frightening, but treatment can improve their symptoms over time.

- You should seek therapy if you are suffering from significant stress or feelings of anxiety or depression. You should choose a different therapist than the one your loved one is seeing.

How Is BPD Treated?

Historically, borderline personality disorder has been challenging to treat. Nevertheless, with newer, evidence-based treatment, people with BPD can suffer fewer and milder symptoms, improved functioning, and a better quality of life.

However, effective treatment requires patience, commitment, and time. Psychotherapy is one form of therapy, while medications can also be used.

If you are very distressed or at risk of harming yourself or others, your healthcare provider may recommend a short-term hospital stay. You will develop a treatment plan with your mental health professional during your stay.

If you also have a co-existing condition, you'll need treatment for it as well.

Other mental health conditions often accompany BPD, such as

- Mood disorders

- Anxiety disorders

- Substance use disorders

- Eating disorders

- Attention-deficit/hyperactivity disorder (ADHD)

- Bipolar disorders

Psychotherapy

Psychological treatment can help you learn skills to manage and cope with your condition. It is possible to improve your self-esteem and live a more rewarding, stable life with treatment.

The following are the most well-known interventions for BPD:

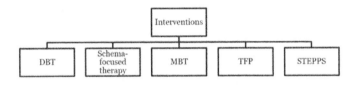

- Dialectical Behavior Therapy (DBT)

DBT is an intervention specifically designed to treat borderline personality disorder. It includes individual therapy, group therapy, and group support for professionals.

Using a skills-based approach, you will learn how to manage your emotions, tolerate distress, and improve relationships.

□Dialectic behavior therapy takes a different and unique approach compared to other cognitive-behavioral therapies that focus on replacing negative behaviors with positive ones. As Dr. Linehan understood, changing her clients' behaviors alone would not be enough to help them.

The term dialectical in DBT describes the core concept of the therapy — the balance of opposites. In other words, the therapy aims to achieve a dynamic balance between *accepting* yourself and embracing *change*.

Dialectic behavior therapy focuses on helping you to accept the reality of life and your behaviors. It promotes change while letting go of unhelpful behaviors. It teaches skills to help you control intense emotions, reduce self-destructive behaviors, and improve relationships.

- Schema-Focused Therapy

Schema-focused therapy is a method of treating consolidated chronic psychological disorders considered hard to treat (like BPD).

The therapy combines cognitive-behavioral therapy with other types of psychotherapy aimed at changing how people see themselves and promoting a positive, healthy lifestyle. The process can be performed individually or in groups.

One of the most successful characteristics of schema therapy is that it offers an integration framework for both the therapist and the patient. Using this framework, they can organize and understand self-defeating patterns of thinking, behaving, feeling, and relating to others. Schemas such as these are called "early dysfunctional schemas."

This approach assumes that borderline personality disorder is caused by a dysfunctional self-image induced by adverse childhood experiences. A dysfunctional self-image impacts how people react, interact, and deal with their environment, problems, and stress.

- Mentalization-Based Therapy (MBT)

Developed to address BPD, MBT relies heavily on attachment theory. Mentalization is at the center of the treatment, and it refers to identifying your thoughts and feelings at any given moment, creating an alternate perspective on the situation.

This program aims to promote self-awareness in relationships of affection: family sessions, group sessions, and individual psychotherapy sessions.

The goal is to maximize and favor the use of your mentalization abilities. This is done by optimizing and promoting your relationship with other family members, your own experience, and others, especially in difficult situations. It involves understanding your own emotions and feelings.

Insecure emotions and thoughts, specifically disorganized style, dominate the stories told by people with BPD. By connecting feelings with thoughts, people with borderline personality disorder can achieve more appropriate behavior; relationships with others can be more satisfying.

- Systems Training for Emotional Predictability and Problem-Solving (STEPPS)

STEPPS is a cognitive-behavioral treatment for people who suffer emotional dysregulation that lasts for 20 weeks. The program is designed for people with difficulty managing intense or changing emotional states.

As part of the therapy, you will work with your family members, caregivers, friends, or significant others in a group setting. This method of treatment is used in addition to other types of psychotherapy.

STEPPS consists of essential skills and advanced emotional and behavioral regulation skills.

- Transference-Focused Psychotherapy (TFP)

TFP aims to help you understand your emotions and interpersonal difficulties by developing a relationship with your therapist.

Through the process, you develop a stable sense of identity. Gaining these insights allows you to manage future interactions outside therapy more effectively.

In the early stages of treatment, the main goal is to reduce the most severe and self-destructive symptoms. Throughout the treatment, you will gain a greater sense of control over your own emotions. Thus, you can maintain more satisfying relationships and ultimately help attain your life goals.

Medication

While the FDA has approved no drugs for treating borderline personality disorder at this time, some medicines may help with symptoms or co-occurring conditions such as depression, impulsivity, aggression, or anxiety. For example, an antidepressant or mood stabilizer can help with mood swings and dysphoria. It may also be helpful for some individuals to take low-dose antipsychotic medication to control symptoms such as disorganized thinking. Make sure to discuss the benefits and potential side effects of these drugs with your doctor.

Hospitalization

Hospitalization is highly recommended when patients have disorder comorbidity, few personal resources, and little support from their environment. This often involves a history of attempted suicide and drug or alcohol abuse. Sometimes, you may need more intensive treatment in a psychiatric hospital or clinic.

Most importantly, be patient with yourself! Recovery takes time. Learning how to manage your emotions, thoughts, and behaviors takes time. Symptoms may be better or worse at different times. Despite this, treatment can help you feel better and function more effectively.

LIFE BEFORE AND AFTER HELP
[Benjamin]

I was diagnosed with borderline personality disorder when I was 28. At that age, I had already attempted suicide three times.

Since my adolescence, I've tried many psychotherapies. Getting my BPD diagnosis was vital in looking for the correct help, which in my case, was DBT. DBT changed the way I look at life. I discovered that most of the time, my suffering came from my perspective on the things that happen and not from the actual events. I learned skills to cope with the intense feelings I experienced without hurting myself or losing sight of my goals.

The essential lesson DBT taught me was that I am worthy of love and capable of change. It might seem simple, but DBT therapists sincerely believed in me, and that was something I had never felt before. Their genuine way of guiding me was inspiring and convinced me that the effort I had to invest in getting better was worth it.

When I was discharged, I spent almost two years without therapy, and last year I returned to an association that specifically treats BPD. With help, it can get better. As a result of psychological care, I have gained the tools to face my life and pursue the goals I thought were impossible.

There are several ways to treat BPD, contrary to its reputation as an incurable condition. You can manage your symptoms and find peace, energy, and resiliency to live better.

TAKEAWAYS

- Early detection and treatment for people with BDP can reduce the severity of their symptoms and improve their psychosocial functioning.

- Mindfulness, distress tolerance skills, and validating environments can help prevent the disorder from fully developing.

- It is time to see a doctor if the symptoms affect your quality of life (eating disorders, sleep problems, significant depression, anger, anxiety, mood swings, and thoughts of suicide or death).

- To diagnose borderline personality disorder, a mental health interview is required.

- Psychological treatment can help you learn skills to manage and cope with your condition:

  - Dialectical behavior therapy (DBT): achieve a dynamic balance between accepting yourself and embracing change.

  - Schema-focused therapy: change how you see yourself and promote a positive, healthy lifestyle.

  - Mentalization-based therapy (MBT): promote self-awareness in relationships of affection to maximize and favor the use of your mentalization abilities.

  - Systems training for emotional predictability and problem-solving (STEPPS): essential skills, as well as advanced emotional and behavioral regulation skills, are taught.

- Transference-focused psychotherapy (TFP): gain a greater sense of control over your own emotions to build more satisfying relationships and attain your life goals.

• Medication may help with symptoms or co-occurring disorders such as depression, impulsivity, aggression, or anxiety.

• It may be necessary to hospitalize people at risk of self-injury or if they have suicidal thoughts.

• Recovery takes time, but there are many ways to learn how to manage your symptoms and find peace, energy, and resilience.

Chapter Four
Taking Care of Your Tulip

"An award-winning rose gardener decides to plant tulips in his garden. He doesn't realize that tulips and roses have different growth requirements. If he treats the tulips like his roses, the tulips won't be able to flourish."

The "Tulip in the Rose Garden"[16] metaphor helps us better understand the role of regulation in borderline personality disorder. Emotionally vulnerable people are the tulips in this metaphor. When people have difficulty managing their emotions, providing the right tools and care will help them thrive in a supportive environment. If the conditions are not correct, they are likely going to struggle.

If the gardener used the same techniques with tulips as with roses, he would probably conclude that tulips have a problem. Similarly, people with BPD require a different treatment plan to bloom.

As discussed in previous chapters, those with borderline personality disorder are not just genetically susceptible to emotions; they have also grown up in an invalidating environment (we could say they have been treated like roses for a long time). Consequently, most of them have not learned how to regulate their emotions, or worse, have never even been aware of their feelings.

People with BPD struggle with emotional regulation. Their difficulty with this skill results from various factors, including intense emotional arousal, problems identifying strong emotions, and the inability to make wise decisions when complicated feelings are present.

What Is Emotional Regulation?

Take some time to reflect on your day and each event you went through. You may have driven to work and experienced a traffic jam that made you angry or frustrated. You might have had a hard day at work. Now, pause for a moment and observe your reactions. Were there any challenging situations at work? Were there any unfair comments from your boss or a co-worker you did not like? In what ways did you deal with today's challenging situations? Did you overreact to the other drivers or to your boss? Your ability to regulate your emotions may have prevented you from doing so, which means you **can** recognize how you feel and respond appropriately.

People are constantly controlling how they respond to emotions. Sometimes they regulate effectively, and sometimes they struggle. People who live with borderline personality disorder usually wrestle with emotional regulation. This means they engage in ineffective regulatory behaviors (such as addictions or self-harm) to feel they are in control of their emotions. Still, the reality is that these regulatory behaviors usually create more problems than provide solutions. Learning to regulate your emotions effectively is an ability that involves identifying, understanding, and accepting emotional experiences.

Regulating emotions can occur before, during, or after a difficult time. This means that emotional regulation can be present at different stages of our situations. For instance, imagine a person struggling with social anxiety. When receiving an invitation to a party, he may feel anxious and start drinking to calm down the stress. To manage his anxiety and fears during the event, the person may consume a lot of alcohol or tell inappropriate jokes, making people uncomfortable. Once home, the same individual may watch TV instead of sleeping to recover for the next workday to distract himself from feeling frustrated about his behavior at the party. He exhibits all these behaviors as he copes with the complex emotions he experiences at different moments.

The skill of regulating emotions is developed during childhood. As we grow up, we learn strategies for coping with distress and understand how to decode our feelings. This process can be negatively affected by the following:

- Childhood stress or trauma

- Punitive or controlling parents

- Differences in brain structure

- Invalidating parenting (parents dismissing, delegitimizing, or communicating that someone's feelings, thoughts, or actions are irrational)

Why Is Emotional Regulation So Important?

Emotional regulation plays a significant role in how you react to events and the people around you. Emotional regulation skills are the pillars of behaving appropriately when distressed and using healthy strategies to manage uncomfortable emotions.

During emotional stress, people who lack emotional regulation skills struggle to control the urges to self-harm, act recklessly, or get aggressive. This is common among people who have borderline personality disorder.

How BPD Affects Emotional Regulation

People with borderline personality disorder experience intense emotions and have trouble regulating them. Consequently, their attempts to manage their feelings are usually not adaptive, harmful to their health, or in conflict with their goals. Someone with this disorder might engage in self-harming behaviors to cope with anxiety and sadness or isolate themself to escape from feeling socially anxious. Drinking, gambling, and other addictive behaviors are also ways of regulating emotions in a dysfunctional way.

Causes of Emotional Arousal Among People With BPD

Imagine you have a cut on your hand. Even though your cut heals, the scarred tissue is extra sensitive since the skin around the wound does not heal properly. The pain peaks every time you touch the area because it feels like the wound tears open again and again. In many ways, this experience resembles that of people with BPD who deal with the world daily and experience emotional sensitivity.

As emotions are perceived intensely, people with BPD react strongly and have difficulty calming down. Here are the three stages of emotional processing:

- Emotional Sensitivity

People with BPD may have emotional reactions that seem to come out of nowhere. Regardless of whether they recognize the trigger or not, they typically react strongly.

- Emotional Reactivity

In addition to having deep sensitivities, such as turning sadness into despair or anger into rage, BPD behavior is also intense and inappropriate for the situation. Both extreme positive and negative emotions are included in this category. Expressing emotional reactivity may be outward or inward, resulting in self-destructive behavior. Examples of emotional reactivity are screaming in public, sleeping for days, or self-harming.

- Slow Return to Baseline

Additionally, people with borderline personality disorder have difficulty calming down, resulting in them staying upset for longer periods than they would like. Regaining your sense of self may take hours or days.

As BPD is characterized by emotional dysregulation, symptoms like unstable relationships and risky or impulsive behavior will be present in related situations.

When you regulate emotions, you can navigate setbacks; however, someone who experiences emotional dysregulation will have trouble understanding their feelings as well as responding to them effectively. This is especially important in BPD since people with the condition often experience significant distress in emotional situations.

For example, a person with emotional regulation skills may feel sad and somewhat depressed following a breakup. However, they will still be able to carry on with their daily routine.

In contrast, someone with BPD going through the same situation may become severely depressed. They may cope by engaging in destructive or violent behaviors or impulsive activities like promiscuity or excessive drinking.

What Does Emotional Dysregulation Look Like in BPD?

As previously mentioned, emotional regulation plays a role in each day-to-day interaction. Therefore, if you have difficulty managing emotions, you will likely experience challenges in various aspects of your life, such as interpersonal relationships, communication, or overcoming obstacles. People with BPD can cope (ineffectively) with emotions in different ways, resulting in the following scenarios:

- Rapid Mood Swings and Irritability

Emotional sensitivity may drive mood swings and irritability in people struggling with BPD. People with this condition are likely to be more emotionally sensitive, causing them to react intensely and quickly to situations.

In addition to intense mood swings, lacking the tools to respond to challenging situations typically results in anxiety and irritability. The people around you may have trouble understanding what you are going through during these episodes, negatively impacting your relationships.

- Difficulty Controlling Anger

There is no explanation for what can trigger rage in people with borderline personality disorder. Even slight inconveniences can cause extreme reactions, which can lead to potentially destructive or violent behaviors, including self-harm.

A lack of control over anger is strongly linked to emotional dysregulation. Also, the intensity or instability of a relationship might play a role since people in chaotic, unstable relationships are more likely to act aggressively.

- Feelings of Emptiness

BPD is characterized by an insecure self-image, leading to chronic feelings of emptiness. A person with borderline personality disorder may experience difficulties embracing their identity, and they may feel isolated from others as well.

Many adverse effects are associated with a sense of emptiness, including impulsive behaviors, self-harm, and suicide. Additionally, chronic emptiness can lead to loneliness since a person who feels disconnected from others may struggle to maintain friendships.

- Paranoia and Fear of Abandonment

There is a high possibility of paranoia for those suffering from BPD because they often worry about being alone, rejected, or abandoned by those closest to them. They may act obsessively and constantly seek reassurance to avoid feeling hurt or rejected. There is a risk of broken relationships due to many of these behaviors.

Difficulty regulating emotions can cause relationships to become more unstable because of a person's inability to soothe feelings of paranoia or insecurity. This dysregulation can then cause intense emotional outbursts.

Developing Emotional Regulation Skills

Building strong emotional regulation skills is possible in many ways. Self-help techniques like mindfulness and working with professionals are some of the ways to learn how to regulate your emotions:

- Consider Therapy

If you struggle with BPD and emotional regulation, seeing a therapist specializing in this condition might be a good idea. They will have a better understanding of the origins of your emotional struggles. With their help, you can learn how to manage your mood swings and regulate your emotions.

Dialectical behavior therapy (DBT) is particularly beneficial for people with BPD. Through this type of therapy, people with BPD can embrace their thoughts and behaviors, thereby learning how to cope with the disorder's symptoms.

Aside from therapy, there are several approaches you can take by yourself to manage your emotions better.

- Mindfulness of Current Emotions

This means being mindful of current emotions without judging them, inhibiting them, blocking them, distracting from them, or holding onto them. There is a basic idea behind this: when painful or distressing emotions are faced without being associated with negative consequences, we extinguish their ability to stimulate secondary negative emotions.

Whenever distressing feelings arise, judging them as "bad" leads to feelings of guilt, shame, anger, or anxiety. These secondary feelings usually make the distress more intense and tolerance more difficult.

- Check the Facts

In many cases, emotions are reactions to thoughts and interpretations rather than events themselves. Sticking to the facts will help you avoid misinterpreting your current emotions and making assumptions about other people's actions.

Consider the following thought as an example: "I am sad again. Today will be a disaster." The only fact about this thought is that you feel sad. The interpretation is that feeling like this means everything will go wrong today. Describing your inner experience may look something like this: "I feel a heavy sensation on my chest, and I feel like crying. It looks like I feel unfortunate." As you can see, the focus was on the facts, leaving out the interpretations and judgments.

Thinking in a judgmental way increases your negative emotions, which causes more judgment, which triggers more emotional pain, and so on. In other words, judging increases the intensity of your feelings, trapping you in a vicious cycle.

- Expressing Your Emotions Through Writing

This technique can be applied in a variety of ways. You could keep a traditional journal on paper or create an online journal. Some days you may write prose, and other days you may write poetry. Choose whatever suits you best.

Expressive writing will help you to better understand what is happening in your life and process it. Journaling is also helpful for managing intense emotions and taking mental distance before deciding. In addition, sharing your writings with others can give you a sense of social support.

When you write about an event, you do not focus on superficial qualities; instead, you focus on the emotional aspects.

Some questions you can answer are:

- How were you feeling at different points in the event?

- What were you thinking?

- What physical sensations did you have?

- How did this event impact how you see yourself, other people, the world, or your future?

- What does this event mean to you now?

- Take Steps to Manage Your Stress

Live a lifestyle that promotes relaxation and self-soothing if you can. You can flourish emotionally by taking care of your body. This might seem unrelated, but we are a unique system in which our emotions and biology are closely linked.

Some supportive activities may include:

- Sleeping 7 to 8 hours a night

- Consuming foods that are nutrient-dense and unprocessed

- Preventing blood sugar dips by eating regularly

- Exercise for 30 minutes a day, five times a week

- Getting support from your pets and family

- Taking advantage of the sunshine by spending time outside

- Using relaxation or mindfulness techniques to manage stress

Some Ideas to Practice Your Mindfulness and Relaxation Skills

Practicing mindfulness implies accepting internal experiences, being able to regulate emotions and moods, thinking flexibly, and approaching problems from a healthy place of acceptance. You can practice mindfulness in the following ways.

- Body Scan

This practice can help you with three things:

1. Providing muscle relaxation and stress relief

2. Feeling more mentally calm and refreshed

3. Helping you reconnect with your body so you better recognize what it needs

You will practice the first "WHAT" skill, which is to **observe**. Using a timer, you will focus on three different zones of your body. This exercise aims to connect with whatever sensations the zone offers; no judging, no analyzing, just noticing. You will feel your shoulders and neck hurt from using the computer, or if you feel hungry. If the urge can wait, return your attention to observing after letting the thought go.

	Step 1	Step 2	Step 3
Area of focus	Feet (toes, soles), ankles, legs, knees, thigh, pelvic area.	Stomach, lower back, chest, upper back, arms, elbows, hands.	Shoulders, neck, face (chin, mouth, nose, eyes, ears, forehead), head, hair.
Duration	5 minutes	5 minutes	5 minutes

- Mindful Breathing

This exercise is powerful, grounding, and practical. When you are anxious or panicking, you must be mindful of your breath. If your mind is clouded with stressful thoughts, focus on your breathing. Taking the time to breathe feels like returning to something familiar and grounding since breathing is inherent to our body.

Start by settling into a comfortable position and allow your eyes to close or keep them open with a softened gaze.

Begin by taking several long slow deep breaths, breathing in fully, and exhaling fully. Breathe in through your nose and out through your mouth.

Allow your breath to find its natural rhythm. Bring your full attention to noticing each in-breath as it enters your nostrils, travels down to your lungs, and causes your belly to expand. Observe each out-breath as your belly contracts and air moves up through the lungs back out through your mouth. Invite your full attention to flow with your breath.

Notice how the inhale is different from exhaling. You may experience the air as feeling cool as it enters your nose and warm as you exhale. As you turn inward, begin to let go of noises around you. If you are distracted by sounds in the room, simply notice them, and bring your intention back to your breath; simply breathe as you breathe, not striving to change anything about your breath. Do not try to control your breath in any way. Observe and accept your experience at this moment without judgment, paying attention to each inhale and exhale.

If your mind wanders to thoughts, plans, or problems, simply accept your mind wandering. Picture the idea as it enters your awareness, and practice letting go of that thought. Then bring your attention back to your breath. Your breath is an anchor you can return to when you become distracted by thoughts repeatedly.

Recognize when your mind has wandered. Observe the types of thoughts that distract you; noticing is the most powerful part of learning. With this knowledge, you can strengthen your ability to detach from thoughts and mindfully focus your awareness back on the qualities of your breath. Practice coming back to the breath with your full attention. Watching the gentle rise of your stomach on the in-breath and the relaxing, letting go on the out-breath.

Allow yourself to focus wholly on your breath as it flows in and out. You may become distracted by pain, discomfort in the body, twitching, or itching sensations that draw your attention away from the breath. You may also notice feelings, perhaps sadness or happiness, frustration, or contentment. Acknowledge whatever comes up, including thoughts or stories about your experience. Notice where your mind went without judging it, pushing it away, clinging to it, or wishing it were different, and simply refocus your mind and guide your attention back to your breath.

Breathe in and breathe out.

Your breath is always with you as a refocusing tool to bring you back to the present moment. As this practice comes to its end, slowly allow your attention to expand over your entire body. When you are ready, open your eyes.

Set a goal to use this practice throughout your day to help cultivate and strengthen attention.

Beyond Thoughts and Emotions

A mental condition like borderline personality disorder profoundly affects emotional regulation, as described in this chapter; however, there is something most people do not realize when it comes to this condition. In addition to the mental and emotional symptoms that a person suffering from BDP experiences, physical symptoms can also manifest.

TAKEAWAYS

- Emotional Regulation

  - This ability involves identifying, understanding, and accepting emotions.

  - People are constantly regulating their emotions, sometimes effectively, sometimes not. Sometimes effectively and adaptively, and sometimes not.

  - Regulation is a skill developed during childhood, and it can be negatively affected by childhood stress or trauma, punitive or controlling parents, and invalidating parenting.

- People with borderline personality disorder experience intense emotions and have trouble regulating them. Consequently, their attempts to manage feelings are typically not adaptive, harmful to personal health, or in conflict with goals.

  - Emotional processing has different stages in BDP:

    - Emotional sensitivity: emotions seem to come out of nowhere, so the individual reacts strongly.

    - Emotional reactivity: the behavior is intense and inappropriate for the situation.

    - Slow return to baseline: the individual has difficulty calming down; it may take hours or days.

- People with BPD can suffer from rapid mood swings and irritability, difficulty controlling anger, feelings of emptiness, paranoia, and fear of abandonment.

- You can develop emotional regulation skills with practices such as:

  ○ Mindfulness of current emotions: You extinguish the secondary negative emotions without judging the situation.

  ○ Check the facts: avoiding misinterpretation and assumptions.

  ○ Expressing your emotions through writing will help you understand what is happening in your life.

  ○ A lifestyle that promotes relaxation and self-soothing.

- Emotional regulation relies on mindfulness. Body scan and mindful breathing can help you improve your mindfulness and relaxation skills.

Chapter Five

Taking Care of Your Body to Manage BPD

Throughout your life, you have probably seen many health specialists. Whether it was a stomach issue, a rash, or a dental emergency, a doctor may have had just the right diagnosis and related treatment.

The first specialists that came to mind when discussing borderline personality disorder are those involved with mental health: psychologists and psychiatrists. However, BPD goes beyond the mental arena; it requires us to consider our physical health.

There is a close connection between the mind and body, and both are deeply affected by one another. In a study [4] conducted in 2020, for example, it was proven there was a link between BPD and physical health issues, such as cardiovascular disease.

When dealing with mental health struggles, a healthy body plays a more critical role than we think. Taking care of the body's most basic physical needs can help the body cope with BPD. You will be able to regulate your emotions and make healthy behavioral decisions when these needs are met.

Managing your BPD symptoms will be much easier if you understand physical well-being.

Overlap of Emotional and Physical Pain

Unlike what most people believe, there is no "pain center" in the brain; feeling pain is a complex experience that involves different processes. A few of these techniques are simple, such as locating discomfort and determining its qualities (if it is piercing, hot, intermittent, for example). Other processes involve linking memories to pain or emotional responses, beliefs about managing it, or creating a plan for managing pain.

Therefore, distressing cognitive responses, such as catastrophizing ("I cannot handle this pain; it will not go away!") and emotional responses, such as depression and anxiety, worsen pain severity.

Additionally, they can hinder your ability to stick with a pain management plan that requires patience and persistence.

The relationship between thoughts, feelings, and physical sensations is not just one-way. While physical pain increases distressing thoughts or emotions and impairs coping, painful thoughts or feelings and poor coping strategies are linked to worsening physical pain. As a result, employing adaptive coping strategies such as healthy eating, exercise, stress management, and treating any mental health issues can reduce pain and improve overall well-being.

BPD and Physical Illness

To this point, it has been well-established that people with borderline personality disorder have difficulty managing their intense emotions and behaviors. But what about the physical impact of this condition? People with BPD tend to notice and focus on the mental and emotional signs, but the mind and body are so closely connected that many also experience unpleasant physical symptoms. Here are some physical symptoms of borderline personality disorder:

- Rashes or Worsened Skin Conditions

There is a strong correlation between BPD, stress, and irritability. As a result of prolonged exposure to these two states, the body produces stress hormones, including cortisol, adrenaline, and norepinephrine. The overproduction of cortisol suppresses the immune system, which in turn causes or worsens skin conditions such as eczema or other rashes.

When you have borderline personality disorder, you are more likely to experience hives, itching, and stinging due to increased stress levels.

- Gut and Digestive Issues

The gastrointestinal tract is sensitive to emotions and mental illness. Anxiety, sadness, anger, or excitement trigger symptoms in the gut; your gut can send signals to your brain and vice versa. Sometimes, the stomach is referred to as our "second brain." An anxious mind can cause digestive distress, exacerbating your mental and emotional symptoms.

When you suffer from BPD, you are likely to have fluctuating emotions, leading to altered bowel habits such as constipation or diarrhea. Also, having borderline personality disorder increases your susceptibility to stomach ulcers because stress diminishes the substances that typically protect you from stomach acid's harmful effects.

- Sensory Block due to Dissociation

In BPD, dissociation can be used to manage pain. This mental process involves disconnection from memories, feelings, thoughts, actions, surroundings, or sense of identity. If you experience this involuntary detachment from reality, it can obstruct your hearing or impair your peripheral vision. It can also affect perception and contribute to memory loss, disrupting the daily functioning of individuals suffering from BPD.

- Constant Fatigue

Borderline personality disorder is highly comorbid with depression, which causes fatigue. With BPD, a person experiences extreme emotional states. Episodes of depression can last for a few hours or several days and can be physically and emotionally draining.

- Hypervigilance

When someone has lived through trauma, hypervigilance can put them on high alert, even during safe times.

- Muscle Aches and Pain

Muscle aches and pain are also common physical symptoms of stress and anxiety. The rapid cycling of moods associated with BPD often causes high emotional stress, which in turn can cause these symptoms.

If you have borderline personality disorder, do not underestimate how emotional swings may affect your body. To help determine if your physical symptoms are related to your mental health disorder, speak to your doctor or mental health provider.

As Albert Einstein once said, "a clever person solves the problem; a wise person avoids it."[17] The best way to improve your health is to take care of your basic needs, make healthier decisions, and be less vulnerable to emotional disruptions.

Focusing On Your Body

Physical and emotional health are closely related, as previously discussed. An unhealthy body will make it difficult for you to manage your emotions.

Dialectic behavioral therapy (DBT) uses the acronym PLEASE to remind people about strategies that can improve emotional regulation based on the importance of this connection between mind and body.

PL	**Treat Physical Illness** Take care of your body responsibly. If necessary, see a doctor and commit to prescribed medication (if there is one).
E	**Balance Your Eating** Be mindful about what you eat, don't eat too much or too little. Eat regularly and choose nutritional food.
A	**Avoid Mind-Altering Substances** Stay off illicit drugs, and if you use alcohol, do it in moderation.
S	**Get Enough Sleep** Ideally, you should sleep 7–9 hours a night. Sleep consistently, especially if you have trouble sleeping.
E	**Get Regular Exercise** Try to do at least 20 minutes of daily exercise.

PL: Treat Physical Illness

Keeping your physical health in check can be as simple as remembering to take your prescribed medications daily. If you have not done this in a while, you should see your doctor about any symptoms you may be experiencing and get tests done if necessary. Treating any physical illness underlying your mental illness will most likely pay off in the long run.

E: Balance Your Eating

Unfortunately, experiencing anxiety and depression can make it difficult for people to eat healthy meals regularly. As difficult as it may be, eating a balanced diet is essential to the PLEASE skill. Imagine that your body is a car. It will go a long way if you put good gas in it, but if you fuel up with bad stuff, it will probably not run well. Giving your body the necessary nourishment improves your ability to cope and regulate emotions.

Following a strict diet plan or doing anything drastic to eat a balanced diet is unnecessary. Instead, start with small steps. Make one healthy swap in your routine, such as taking a multivitamin or adding more fruit daily. You can achieve a well-balanced diet by adding small changes over time.

According to specialists[5] mood disorders can be prevented and treated through your diet by eating whole foods such as the following:

- Foods rich in omega-3 help reduce inflammation and promote brain health. The best omega-3 foods include wild-caught salmon, mackerel, herring, white fish, walnuts, chia seeds, flaxseeds, natto, and egg yolks.

- Fruits and vegetables contain antioxidants and vital nutrients that support your mood and prevent deficiencies. A good diet should include leafy greens like spinach and kale, avocado, asparagus, beets, broccoli, carrots, peppers, tomatoes, mushrooms, blueberries, goji berries, blackberries, cranberries, and artichokes.

- Healthy fats provide essential vitamins and minerals that boost energy levels and mood. The best options are avocados, grass-fed butter, coconut oil, extra virgin olive oil, and omega-3s such as walnuts and flaxseeds. You should avoid trans fats (like hydrogenated oils) and processed vegetable oils, which can cause inflammation in the body.

- Protein sources support neurological function and hormone balance, which are essential. Protein-rich foods include grass-fed beef, lentils, wild fish, organic chicken, black beans, yogurt, free-range eggs, raw cheese, and bone broth-based protein powder.

- Probiotic foods support gut health, cognitive function, and neurotransmitter production. These types of foods include kefir, yogurt, kombucha, miso, raw cheese, and fermented vegetables. Drinking kombucha daily is a great way to consume probiotics, as it also contains enzymes and B vitamins that boost your energy levels.

A: Avoid Mind-Altering Substances

Unless prescribed by a doctor, mind-altering substances should not be used by people with mental health disorders like borderline personality disorder. These substances include:

- Alcohol

- Caffeine

- Nicotine

- Medications prescribed to other people

- Illegal drugs

You may not be able to apply coping mechanisms effectively if you partake in mind-altering substances. An expert can help you stop using substances.

S: Get Enough Sleep

The effects of a poor sleep cycle can be detrimental to your physical health. It is common for some people to get too little sleep, while others can get too much, especially those with disorders like depression. You need to find a healthy balance for your mind to regulate emotions effectively.

The following guidelines can help you maintain good sleep hygiene:

- Avoid using your phone for at least 30 minutes before bed.

- Maintain a regular sleep routine.

- Daytime naps should be avoided (or shortened to less than 30 minutes).

- Don't watch TV, use the computer, or read in bed.

- Drink caffeinated drinks with caution.

- Avoid inappropriate substances that interfere with sleep.

- Get some exposure to daylight during waking hours.

- Optimize your bedroom for restful sleep.

Other behaviors, like the next PLEASE skill, can also help you sleep better.

E: Get Regular Exercise

A decade of research supports the health benefits of regular exercise on both a mental and physical level. In addition to treating underlying physical illnesses, it can improve moods and regulate sleeping patterns.

Every individual has a different idea of what enough exercise is. For some people, running marathons or cycling 20 miles a day is ideal; for others, playing with their pets is sufficient. You can see profound benefits from walking every day if you have not exercised in a while.

Running as Therapy

In Canada, mental health professionals have developed a treatment.[6] based on running as the primary skill for managing other symptoms of borderline personality disorder. The BPD Treatment Program conducts a nine or ten-week running program each year for fifteen to seventeen patients of varying ages. During the week, participants attend two running practices and must complete one more on their own. Ultimately, the program aims for participants to complete a five-kilometer race, typically the Epic Canadian Run for Canada, in July. The goal is for the participants to become familiar with habitual exercise and gain the confidence to exercise independently.

Preliminary results are promising after four years of the program. Various pre- and post-tests showed that participants' moods changed for the better post-exercise, and the professional team hopes to demonstrate that higher-intensity exercise has a more significant effect.

An impressive aspect of the program is that it has a low dropout rate, with only one to three participants dropping out each cycle. This is because the program is a group environment, which keeps people more accountable, builds confidence, and reduces low self-esteem about exercise, especially if they are nervous.

Additionally, participants are offered incentives as part of the program. BPD Treatment Program partners with the Mental Health Foundation and Aerobics First, a fitness clothing and gear store that provides free shoe fittings and running shoes to those who complete five running practices.

Runners can also enjoy guest speakers as incentives. Nutritionists, physiotherapists, academics, and others speak with the participants about the benefits of exercise and good nutrition. Additionally, veterans of past running programs often mentor and motivate current participants.

As people with borderline personality disorder experience highs and lows very frequently, habitual exercise has the potential to help regulate moods and help them cope with their disorder. Therefore, running is an essential component of their treatment plan.

In addition to the above, the following activities are recommended:

- Yoga

Yoga is an excellent way to stretch and move your body on a low-impact basis. In addition to lowering blood pressure and reducing anxiety, it helps with breathing and calming the mind. BPD, anxiety, and depression treatment centers often include yoga in their recovery programs because yoga is so beneficial to mental health.

- Swimming

Swimming is an ideal low-impact exercise. You can increase your endurance, flexibility, and muscle strength by floating in the water, which puts less stress on your body, bones, and joints. Furthermore, swimming is a fun and relaxing exercise that can be done in a group or individually.

Where Do I Start?

It is normal to feel overwhelmed by the number of disciplines available: yoga, spinning, aerobics, pickleball, pilates, running, or weightlifting. No matter what, there is sure to be one that suits your needs. Once you decide what you want to do, a workout plan is the best way to stay committed. A fitness planner is something you may want to invest in to help you stay consistent. Below is a sample fitness planner:

Fitness Planner

Date : _____		Water : ●●●●●●○○	
Breakfast	Lunch	Dinner	Snack

Resistance Training			
Exercise	Set	Rep	Weight

Cardio			
Exercise	Time	Dist.	Cal.	Heart rate

Physical health affects your overall health, as well as your self-esteem and relationships, therefore taking care of your body is essential.

Do not underestimate the power of self-care. Health problems, even minor ones, can interfere with or overshadow other aspects of your life. You can feel stressed and unhappy even if you suffer from minor health problems like aches and pains, lethargy, and indigestion.

In addition, poor health habits can increase your stress levels and affect your ability to cope with other BPD symptoms.

Borderline personality disorder symptoms are detrimental to your mental, emotional, and physical well-being and impact your relationships. Having trouble forming relationships is one of the hallmarks of BPD, as discussed earlier. However, it is not entirely hopeless. Keep reading to learn how to manage your interactions.

TAKEAWAYS

- There is a two-way relationship between thoughts, feelings, and physical sensations. The presence of physical pain leads to distressing thoughts and emotions. It also impairs coping with painful feelings. Poor coping strategies worsen physical pain.

- People with BPD tend to notice and focus on the mental and emotional symptoms, but the mind and body are so closely connected that many also experience unpleasant physical symptoms. Some of them are:

  - Rashes or worsened skin conditions

  - Gut and digestive issues

  - Sensory block due to dissociation

  - Constant fatigue

  - Hypervigilance

  - Muscle aches and pain

- Physical and emotional health are closely related. An unhealthy body will make it difficult for you to manage your emotions.

- Dialectic behavioral therapy (DBT) uses the acronym PLEASE to remind people about strategies that can improve emotional regulation based on the importance of this connection between mind and body.

- PL: Treat physical illness

- E: Balance your eating

- A: Avoid mind-altering substances

- S: Get enough sleep

- E: Get regular exercise

- Physical well-being can be enhanced by running, yoga, and swimming.

- A workout plan you can stick to is the best way to stay consistent in your exercise.

Chapter Six

Dealing with Others Amid Your Inner Battles

There is no doubt that building a relationship is essential to living a quality life. Love is an engine of great joy but can also cause moments of suffering. Regarding relationships, the intuitive insights of people without borderline personality disorder may not be so evident to those struggling with BPD on a daily basis. A person who suffers from BPD may have many questions regarding their relationships with others. "What is expected in human interactions?" "How do I build healthy relationships?" "How can I deal with emotional dependencies?"

The desire to have good relationships with our friends and loved ones is natural, as we all want to feel good and grow as individuals, which we achieve through relationships. This can be challenging at times and in certain stages of life. Intimate relationships, for example, exist between two people who enter a path of life together while maintaining their individuality, generating good communication, and respect between them. Working together and having plasticity in negotiating agreements, all without being selfish, are necessary for sustaining a successful relationship.

People who have been diagnosed with BPD feel emotional instability and impulsiveness. It is also typical for them to have distorted images of themselves, their goals, and their internal preferences. For this reason, they can immediately give their attention and affection and be passionate in their relationships. For someone with BPD, this can happen without measuring the emotional intensity. As a result, they can often feel intense discomfort, irritability, or anguish if there are negative consequences.

In addition, people diagnosed with borderline personality disorder may have a deep fear of abandonment or even of getting too close to people because of insecure early bonds or traumatic experiences.

Here are some eye-opening statistics[7] about BPD sufferers' relationships:

- According to studies on individuals aged around 40, 60% of borderline personality disorder patients are married. The number is fewer than the general population (in the United States, 85% of people are married by age 40.)

- People with BPD do not have higher divorce rates than the general population. By the average age of around 40, the divorce rate for people with BPD is near 35%, and this is comparable to the divorce rate for the average U.S. citizen.

- People with borderline personality disorder are far less likely to remarry after a divorce. Only about 10% of people with BPD get remarried by around age 40, which is nearly half the national remarriage rate.

- Those with BPD who recover from their symptoms are more likely to marry and become parents and are less likely to divorce or lose custody.

As you can see from the data above, a significant aspect of borderline personality disorder is struggling with relationships. You probably already know this if you or a close friend have been diagnosed with BPD.

Why Do People with BPD Struggle In Relationships?

Data shows that attachment style can become a stumbling block for people with BPD regarding relationships[8]. In addition, behaviors and symptoms associated with BPD negatively impact relationships. Here are some reasons behind the data:

- BPD Patients Fear Rejection

Almost everyone who suffers from this disorder will have difficulty holding onto relationships, mainly because of being extra sensitive to rejection. It is common for people with borderline personality disorder to perceive rejection even when it is not intended.

The word **scrutiny** is a valid descriptor of how people with BPD interact with others. It is common for the individual to pay close attention to every detail of a conversation or an interaction, believing that they will be able to determine subtle emotional cues. To control the environment around them, they pay a lot of attention to how people treat them and take their behavior very personally. Feeling rejected creates emptiness, anger, or despair, which they wish to avoid.

As a result, they can either become overly attached to their partner to prevent them from leaving, or they may leave first.

- Unrealistic Expectations

People with borderline personality disorder tend to be in a very vulnerable emotional state and they see relationships as the answer to all their interpersonal and emotional needs. Their expectations do not often match the average person's expectations; They tend to look for "perfect" relationships.

You can imagine how frustrating this is for them. Almost no one lives up to their expectations, which causes burnout, anger, confusion, and misunderstandings among family members and partners.

A study[9] conducted in 2018 compared the relationships of couples where one partner suffered from borderline personality disorder and those where neither had the illness. According to their research, the BPD partner's perception of the relationship was more negative than the partner's, showing that BPD symptoms negatively impacted trust and happiness in romantic relationships.

BPD is sometimes stigmatized as a condition associated with manipulation or selfishness. It is essential to understand that these problematic behaviors are a symptom of the illness, an attempt to meet their emotional and relationship needs.

- Obsessions Are a Big Deal

The obsessions that arise from BPD deeply affect romantic relationships.

People with BPD can 'intend' to spend all their time with their other half, even if it is not practical or desirable.

It is possible for them to feel withdrawn and lonely when away from their partner. Someone who feels this way can escalate into thoughts of self-harm or suicide, making it difficult for the other person to ask for space.

- Arguments Are Never "Little"

No matter who you are, you have likely been in an argument before; thinking differently and trying to reach an agreement is normal. A simple argument, however, can trigger an emotional downward spiral in a relationship when someone has BPD because they perceive it as an indication of abandonment.

In many cases, partners learn this the hard way, making them feel they cannot discuss serious issues without significant conflict.

Partners and family members should be involved in the patient's treatment to learn how to react in certain situations. Family members and friends can also help their loved ones use the skills they learned to help them regulate their emotions and succeed in relationships.

Helping does not mean taking full responsibility. If you are involved with someone who blames you for their emotional state, despite your desire to support them, it is ultimately the patient's responsibility to take care of themselves.

- Having an Impulsive Sexual Nature

People with borderline personality disorder often struggle with sexuality issues; impulsive sexuality is a typical symptom. Furthermore, many people with BPD have been sexually abused as children, making their adult sex lives difficult.

Over the years, studies[10] about sexual behavior have shown that the sexual behavior of those with BPD differs from those without BPD. Those with borderline personality disorder exhibited impulsivity in various ways, such as sexual encounters at a younger age, more casual sexual experiences, and with more partners.

In addition, researchers[11] have found that women with BPD symptoms are more likely to experience unplanned pregnancies.

- Rapid Emotional Changes

Often, BPD has been considered a "black-and-white" condition. People with borderline personality disorder tend to idolize people in certain situations and then devalue them quickly. This makes it hard for them to maintain relationships, career choices, and friendships. The difficulty of living with someone who sees you differently depending on the day is overwhelming, to say the least. Communicating and connecting with your loved one becomes more challenging as their identity and place in the world shift. Relationships can become chaotic, feeling like a rollercoaster with highs and lows.

In addition to this opposing view of people, those with BPD often do not realize they are causing the problem. This makes coping with these pendulum swings especially difficult for friends and loved ones.

When it comes to borderline personality disorder, one may believe that the world is against them, that things never work out for them, and that they cannot get what they want. Since people with BPD often find themselves in the same predicaments repeatedly, therapy is necessary to help navigate out of this cycle.

Understanding that you can have a healthy relationship even if you have a personality disorder is essential. The combination of treatment and a strong support network can lead to a more stable emotional and romantic life.

Even though treatment will not completely cure borderline personality disorder, it can help you cope with the symptoms and respond in less harmful ways to you or your partner. Understanding your attachment style and how it affects your interpersonal relationships is a good start.

Discover Your Attachment Style as a Starting Point

From birth, human beings develop a behavioral pattern called **attachment**, allowing them to relate to others. The first interactions with their parents or caregivers teach them how to relate to others.

In the first years of life, individuals discover the world through sensory perception. You sense and store those memories in implicit memory. Learning to speak means that people continue to learn about the world and others, but now you learn through language and store this knowledge in explicit memory.

People develop patterns from birth to death to relate, connect, and bond with others. First, you learn to communicate through your senses and then through language, allowing you to organize and categorize experiences with others.

You understand emotion regulation better through attachment. The hundreds of interactions you have with those closest to you since birth have taught you how to regulate emotions. This self-regulation and regulation with others are part of your learning history and follow you wherever you go. In many relationships, what you have learned repeats itself many times and organizes a behavioral pattern for you to relate to others in a certain way.

Various life experiences can lead to different attachment styles:

- Anxious attachment style: "It is imperative to me that you like me."

- Disorganized attachment style: "I am attracted to you and not attracted to you."

- Dismissive attachment style: "I do not want to want you."

- Secure attachment: "You are what I want, and I am okay with that."

Many believe that attachment styles are unchangeable and that nothing can be done about them. These learning patterns are rigid, which will cause you to behave the same way repeatedly.

To break out of this rigid pattern, you must learn to pause, notice, and check what matters to you before responding. It takes a little while to practice a new behavior. Still, people with borderline personality disorder are not powerless to learn, especially when facing the consequences of their old ways of relating to others and interacting with their values.

The attachment style can be understood by thinking of it as a deck of cards. Imagine you were given cards outlining how your parents treated you, your upbringing, and your life circumstances. It is not the deck of cards you wanted but what you got. What do you want to do moving forward? How about using the cards given to you to create the relationships you want?

Assessing Your Attachment-Driven Behaviors

You can observe the impact your attachment style has on your relationships by doing this exercise[12].

To begin, think about three relationships to work on for this activity. You are trying to identify what happened that started the old, repetitive behavioral pattern when dealing with others. Linking a trigger, an emotional experience, and a response prevents you from becoming blinded by the idea that difficulty with others is an out-of-the-blue issue.

The second step is to look for familiar emotions that accompany problematic behaviors triggered when interacting with others (such as rejection, anger, disrespect, or feeling attacked).

Close your eyes and concentrate on your breathing for the next few minutes. Next, recall a mildly upsetting memory you had with someone you care about this year that triggered those attachment-driven behaviors, and notice how your body feels.

As you hold this memory in your mind, pay attention to the sensations that arise. Check the intensity of the feeling, the thoughts that pop into your mind, and any go-to actions that come with the memory. What do you feel like doing? Is there any urge to suppress or run away from this feeling? Notice the life of this emotion, how it changes naturally, and how maybe a new sensation comes with it.

Do your best to observe the coming and going of sensations and feelings one by one.

When you are ready, open your eyes and bring your attention back to the present moment. What do you notice if you return to a troublesome situation and intentionally accept an unpleasant feeling? If you would like, you can write down your experience.

Go Beyond the Basics to Build Meaningful Relationships

It is becoming popular to say "neurons that fire together wire together" when talking about brain plasticity. This means that when people behave differently, the brain structure is modified due to multiple learning experiences, leading to new neural maps. In other words, brain architecture continues to change throughout life, even during adulthood.

In short, people with borderline personality disorder can relate to others effectively with the right skills. It does not matter if you grew up in a harsh environment, had a rough learning history, and had your emotional machinery activated daily — you can always change your behavior.

The symptoms and behaviors of BPD can be challenging, especially in relationships. Despite these challenges, you can maintain a healthy and long-lasting relationship — several strategies can help.

Forming stable relationships can be improved when borderline personality disorder is diagnosed and treated early. BPD is rarely treated with medications first. However, a doctor or psychiatrist may prescribe you or your partner medication to control depression, anxiety, and mood swings. In addition to reducing mood swings, medications can also make other interventions more effective, such as therapy.

As mentioned before, psychotherapy is highly recommended for people with borderline personality disorder. In addition to one-on-one therapy, group therapy is also available. Couples therapy may also be beneficial to your relationship.

To avoid burnout or excessive stress, taking proper care of yourself when dealing with BPD in relationships is essential. Several additional ideas can be helpful:

- Avoid isolation by spending time with family and friends who listen to you and care about you.

- Take some time to relax and have fun – it is not selfish to do so. Taking care of yourself and destressing with a hobby you enjoy will improve your relationship.

- Take part in support groups. Talk to people who understand your situation.

- Manage stress and emotional health by eating, exercising, and sleeping well.

Connect with friends or family members by engaging in these self-care ideas:

- Spend time outdoors.

- Make Saturday or Sunday morning brunch together.

- Make a list of things you love about each other.

- Go to a Zumba class.

- Take cooking lessons.

- Workout together.

- Go for a drive or a walk.

- Make vision boards together.

- Go out for a meal or cook together

- Volunteer together.

There is more to borderline personality disorder than just how it affects relationships with family, friends, or romantic partners. BPD patients may also have difficulty maintaining relationships with coworkers, bosses, and other authority figures. As you will see in the next chapter, a person's work or career may also be affected by BPD symptoms.

TAKEAWAYS

- A significant aspect of BPD is struggling with relationships:

  - Fewer BPD patients are married than the general population.

  - People with BPD are far less likely to remarry after a divorce.

  - Those with BPD who recover from their symptoms are more likely to marry and become parents and are less likely to divorce or lose custody.

- Behaviors and symptoms associated with BPD that negatively impact relationships are:

  - Fear of rejection

  - Unrealistic expectations

  - Obsessions

  - Rapid emotional changes

  - Impulsive sexual nature

- Relationships can be complex for people with BPD due to their attachment style. People learn how to relate to others through initial interactions with parents or caregivers. From birth to death, individuals develop patterns of relating, connecting, and bonding with others.

- There are different attachment styles:

- Anxious attachment style

- Disorganized attachment style

- Dismissive attachment style

- Secure attachment

• Multiple learning experiences alter the brain's structure, resulting in new neural maps (brain architecture changes throughout life, even during adulthood).

• People with borderline personality disorder can relate to others effectively with the right skills. To achieve those skills, you can do the following:

- Therapy

- Medication

- Self-care

• It does not matter if you grew up in a harsh environment, had a rough education, or if your emotional machinery is constantly activated; changing your behavior is always possible.

Chapter Seven
Managing BPD at Work

Even though borderline personality disorder is a stigmatized condition, as previously discussed, it is possible to live with this disorder and lead a prosperous professional career. It may not be very easy, but it is possible with the right help and support from your environment.

To achieve success, two things are necessary. First, personal knowledge is required to understand the disorder. Many people may spend their entire life without knowing they have BPD because it is not a well-understood condition. An appropriate diagnosis of this condition will help you understand how it will impact your life, specifically your work reality. Taking the necessary medications and getting psychotherapy can also make a big difference in your work experience.

And second, it is beneficial to have support from the people in your work environment, such as colleagues and employers, as well as from your family and friends. BPD patients often are viewed as manipulative, violent, or impossible to treat, and this kind of judgment makes it more difficult for them to thrive in their vocational careers. The support of your work environment is essential for having professional success.

How BPD Affects Your Work

It is essential to realize how borderline personality disorder can interfere with your chosen career if you wish to succeed. Depending on the workplace settings, BPD can impact how you perform at work, feel about your colleagues, and other aspects of your work environment. As you deal with the effects of BDP in your workplace, it may be difficult to feel fulfilled and purposeful.

Your career can be affected by the following factors:

- Distorted Self-Image

One of the main difficulties people with BPD face is having a distorted view of themselves. You cannot build a meaningful professional career if you do not know how you are. You can easily define your aspirations and the steps necessary to achieve them when you are confident about your identity. As a result, people with borderline personality disorder may find it challenging to work with constancy to achieve their goals.

- All-or-Nothing Thinking

BPD sufferers tend to judge things as black or white, which can be damaging when attempting to build relationships. The same thing goes for the workplace, where observing reality in this way can harm relationships with co-workers. It is tough to achieve empathy when the world is viewed in such static and rigid categories.

- Unstable Relationships

The importance of relationships in the workplace cannot be overstated; a good working relationship with co-workers and superiors is vital. People with borderline personality disorder tend to have unstable relationships, which will undoubtedly complicate their careers. Besides feeling as if they are not in the right place, enjoying everyday life with those around them will also be challenging.

- Dissociation

Dissociation significantly affects professional life since it is complicated to succeed if your mind is not "present." Concentrating on projects will become problematic because they may seem unreal or unfamiliar. You may not recognize the world around you when you feel disconnected from your thoughts, emotions, behaviors, and identity. Professionals might recommend medication or intensive therapy if dissociation is a common occurrence.

- Impulsive Behavior and Mood Swings

Some people with borderline personality disorder make impulsive decisions that can hurt their careers or co-workers. For instance, they may drink excessively, drive recklessly, spend recklessly, or have sex with multiple partners. These behaviors can negatively affect your work, whether you consistently fail to show up on time, make reckless decisions on the job, or develop a toxic working relationship.

- Interpersonal Communication Problems

As a result of borderline personality disorder, one of the most challenging aspects of working is relating to superiors, especially when feeling controlled or smothered by the boss. As discussed previously, your working experience might be affected by the rapid shifts in BPD from idealization to devaluation. Also, the fear of abandonment that causes you to cut off relationships too soon or become involved in intense relationships quickly might interfere.

- Concentration Inabilities

If you have BPD, you will probably find it nearly impossible to work on a specific task because you may quickly feel bored and experience prolonged mood swings. The symptoms of dissociation and derealization can also affect a person's concentration and focus. Hence, you might find it hard to commit to the assigned tasks in the workplace.

Despite all these effects of borderline personality disorder on your work life, you can reduce the symptoms by implementing various techniques. A study from 2019[13] suggests that it is possible to improve success in the workplace for people with BDP, increasing support for employment and addressing stigma.

Some projects, such as The Connections Place[14] program, help people with BPD deal with emotional barriers to prepare for the workplace.

How to Be Successful in the Workplace

While the symptoms of BPD may make things more complicated, it is still possible to have a successful career. The good news is there are some things you can try which could make a significant difference to your situation. You can use different techniques to solve the problems that may arise depending on the circumstances.

- Avoid Stressful Situations

You will likely be exposed to many moments when you feel overwhelmed and anxious. To manage your symptoms successfully at work, you need to learn how to identify these situations and avoid them. For example, ensuring nothing is left unfinished that could cause problems in the future is a way of preventing stress.

- Take Your Medication and Keep Your Appointments.

No matter how well you feel, taking your medication and attending all your doctor appointments is vital. If you are considering stopping or changing your medication, consult your mental health professional first.

With the help of your therapist, find a balance between your scheduled sessions and your work. As well as prescribing medications specific to your symptoms, they can also recommend some lifestyle changes. It would be best to respect their suggestions and not make decisions without consulting them first.

- Try Relaxation Exercises

Practicing deep breathing or meditation can help you overcome stressful situations in your daily life. If you practice mindfulness, you can maintain stability in your work, regardless of the environment.

If you work at home, try the following:

- Ensure you are in a comfortable position before starting.

- Do not focus too intently.

- Play some relaxing music.

- Practice the exercise frequently to get better.

- Spend a little more time with each session.

- Five Tips for Mindful Eating at Work Take time to decide on your meal consciously.

- Eliminate distractions around you.

- Eat your food slowly.

- Rate your hunger before eating.

- Take the opportunity to connect with someone over your meal.

In addition to avoiding stressful situations and committing to your medication and medical appointments, you can also try incorporating little changes into your daily routine. These changes can be divided into two groups. First, there are personal habits you can incorporate at home by yourself. And second, some new practices will help you at work. Since you must work with others, making changes will be challenging but rewarding in the long run.

Changes at Home

- Talk to Someone

In addition to your therapist, it is essential to have someone close who can listen to and support you; they could be an immediate family member or friend. You can feel less alone and better understand your situation by talking with someone.

- Create a Crisis Plan

Make a list of some things you can do when you are not feeling as eager and confident as when you feel at your best. These ideas could be new plans for managing a crisis, such as who to contact or some strategies for self-help.

- Take Care of Your Physical Health

A healthy diet and regular exercise will give you more energy to manage your health problems. Getting enough sleep and staying away from drugs and alcohol are essential. This way, you will have the power and physical health to succeed in your professional projects.

- Give Yourself a Break

People with borderline personality disorder can experience intense feelings when they receive negative feedback or are in conflict with a colleague at work. Give yourself time to process the situation instead of reacting immediately; it will be easier to explain your emotions when you are calm.

You can also manage stress and anxiety at work by taking a break. You may find that regular intervals during the day will help you avoid becoming overworked or always "on." Take some time to do things you enjoy during your lunch break or take a short walk with a colleague; feelings will be easier to deal with if you do this. Once home, taking a walk, watching a movie, listening to music, or exercising are all options to cope with strong emotions from work.

- Keep Track of Your Mood

Keep a daily diary where you can record your mood swings. This will help you gain a better understanding of your feelings as well as the reasons behind them. You can eliminate stress triggers and improve workplace health by mood tracking. While you are handling your own responsibilities, it becomes easy to forget about how you are feeling. Feelings often go unnoticed while you work, but they determine how you act and what you say. Keeping track of your mood throughout the day will allow you to respond appropriately to your emotions.

- Try Peer Support

It might help you feel more supported to connect with others facing similar challenges. In your local area, look for peer support groups and therapeutic communities.

Changes at the Workplace

- Define Work Boundaries

An all-or-nothing mindset can disrupt your work-life balance. You can manage burnout and stress by setting boundaries around your work.

You can set your devices to "do not disturb" or mute notifications until the next day if you find it difficult not to look at emails after work hours. Keep track of your day-to-day tasks by setting timers and alerts and speaking up if you feel your workload is too heavy.

- Write letters but do not send

If you feel intense emotions towards someone at work, try writing a letter to the person without sending it. By doing this, you can feel as if you have expressed yourself. Not sending the letter can help protect your interpersonal relationships.

- Tell Your Boss and Partners About Your Situation

Some people find that being transparent about their borderline personality disorder improves their relationships at work. You do not have to tell your boss that you have BPD, but remember that explaining your mood swings and impulsive behaviors or asking for help may be good for you.

- Ask for Adjustments at Work

To be more productive, you may need to make some changes in your role or work environment.

There is no one-size-fits-all solution for workplace accommodations. Among them could include:

- Flexible work schedule

- Time off for mental health appointments

- Work from home

- Private Office

- Redesign large job tasks into smaller tasks

- Use to-do lists and checklists

- Set long-term and short-term goals with your supervisor

Career Suggestions for People with BPD.

Those who struggle with BPD must consider their circumstances to find a job that is perfect for them. Your career will be more challenging if you suffer from this disorder and lack support at work. It is essential to consider a few factors when deciding what job is best for you. Identifying these characteristics or conditions in your work will enable you to have a more successful career.

By engaging in creative professions that allow you to use your strengths and abilities, you will avoid getting bored so quickly. Therefore, engaging in jobs that include designing, strategizing, organizing, solving problems, and planning is beneficial. In addition, flexible schedules can give you more autonomy in managing your time.

Maintaining your mental health also requires a non-stressful working environment. For you to thrive, knowing where you will work is crucial so that you can receive support from your colleagues and your boss. You may prefer a calm environment without distractions, or you may choose a busy environment where there are a lot of tasks to complete. Knowing your preferences will make finding the right place easier.

You can control your emotions more effectively if you are focused. Finally, to be more productive and maintain your focus, you will also need some structure in your routine. By keeping similar conditions in your work environment over time, you will be able to reduce your impulsive behaviors and fast changes in emotions.

Finding the Perfect Fit

You must consider many career options to manage your symptoms and achieve your goals. Having borderline personality disorder does not mean you cannot have a job that makes you happy.

In this section, you will find a long list with many possibilities to consider, divided into categories to help you quickly identify the ones that appeal to you.

- Creative Jobs

Acting, advertising, marketing, art and design, crafting, tailoring, TV and radio, photography, journalism, writing-related professions, theatrical careers, music, baking.

- Caring Roles

Teaching, social work, nursing, babysitting, animal care.

- Health and Fitness

Personal care aid, massage therapist, nutritionist, yoga teacher, personal trainer.

- Fast Paced

Salesperson, restaurant server, cook, bartender.

- Flexible Schedule

Uber driver, Lyft driver, real estate agent, marketing consultant, personal trainer.

- Low Human Interaction:

Pet sitting, dog walking, dog trainer, pet groomer, gardener, housekeeper, truck driver.

When Choosing a Job, Approach with Caution

While searching for a perfect job, you will likely consider many options; maybe you will find one that was not listed above. This is just a general approach that may be helpful to you. To find a fulfilling career, you must have a great sense of self-knowledge. Knowing your strengths and interests, as well as your limitations and fears will help you decide what type of work is right for you.

Jobs are indeed difficult for people with borderline personality disorder, but some are especially challenging. Therefore, it is essential to be cautious if you are trying to start a job with some of the following characteristics:

- Work environments that require a lot of teamwork and cooperation

- Activities that require an emotional commitment can easily change your mood

- Activities requiring a prolonged period of focus

Some questions to consider when choosing a job.

You can use these questions to guide you when looking for what job suits you, whether you are still in school or looking for a career change.

What activities do you see yourself doing?

What you do in your job (the tasks you perform) are what defines your job. Therefore, thinking about what activities you imagine yourself doing is essential. Nobody says you cannot do a job you don't like if you can adapt. If you do not enjoy what you do, it is probably not your ideal job.

How satisfied are you with your work today?

Since we spend a lot of time working, the more satisfied we are with our work, the happier we will be. Our ideal job can make all the difference when it comes to feeling fulfilled and happy. The person we hope to become often aligns with how we operate as professionals.

Does your job allow you to develop your skills and knowledge?

The best job allows you to develop professionally and personally. You are likely close to the ideal position if the work increases your skills and knowledge. In contrast, if work limits you, it is easy to get bored and feel unproductive.

What working conditions seem most important to you?

Your ideal job is also the one that best suits the working conditions you want. Working with a contract or without it, working ten hours versus eight hours, or doing it with the minimum physical and security conditions all affect your well-being, which is why you should be aware of your job's requirements. The importance placed on these workplace factors will determine whether a specific work is ideal for you or not.

When it comes to your job, what goals do you set for yourself?

Choosing the right job for you depends mainly on your professional goals. The perfect job for someone who is ambitious and wants to develop a professional career will allow them to reach personal goals. If you are not very ambitious and are content with working, regardless of the position, then any job can be your ideal one.

As discussed in the previous chapters, several aspects of a person's life are affected by BPD. You can manage borderline personality disorder with the use of additional self-help techniques.

TAKEAWAYS

- Having borderline personality disorder can have an adverse effect on your career choice. A person suffering from BPD may experience a negative impact on how they perform at work, how they feel about their colleagues, and other aspects of their work environment, according to the circumstances.

- Your career can be affected by distorted self-image, all-or-nothing thinking, unstable relationships, dissociation, impulsive behavior, mood swings, interpersonal communication problems, and concentration inabilities.

- You can still have a successful career if you have BPD. To avoid or solve problems that may arise, you can do the following:

  - Avoid stressful situations.

  - Take your medication and keep your appointments.

  - Change your habits at home. This can involve talking to someone, creating a crisis plan, taking care of your physical health, giving yourself a break, keeping an eye on your mood, or getting peer support.

  - Take steps to improve your workplace, such as setting boundaries, writing letters you don't send, talking to your boss and partners, and asking for adjustments.

- People with borderline personality disorder should consider careers with the following characteristics:

- ○ Creative professions allow you to use your strengths and abilities to avoid getting bored quickly.

- ○ Jobs with flexible schedules can give you more autonomy in managing your time.

- ○ Careers in non-stressful working environments.

- ○ A job with a structured routine will also help you be more productive and maintain concentration.

- Be cautious if you are trying to start a job with some of the following characteristics:

- ○ Work environments that require a lot of teamwork and cooperation.

- ○ Activities that require an emotional commitment can easily change your mood.

- ○ Activities requiring a prolonged period of focus.

Chapter Eight

Living Without Borders - Other Ways to Cope With BPD

Although people often admire and look up to the famous, they struggle with the same life challenges as the rest of the world. Some of these individuals are included with 1.6 percent of the population struggling with BPD. Many famous people have exhibited symptoms of borderline personality disorder over the years, even though it was never officially stated that they had it. A few dealt with abandonment issues, while others attempted suicide or abused drugs and alcohol.

Others like Megan Fox have openly shared their struggles with mental health issues. It is no secret that the talented young actress had a mental illness; her impulsive behavior and emotional instability are all symptoms of borderline personality disorder.

Darrell Hammond is another famous person diagnosed with post-traumatic stress disorder, schizophrenia, and borderline personality disorder. Having been severely abused as a child, the American stand-up comedian, actor, and impressionist fought mental illness for most of his life. In the past, Hammond has spoken about his struggles with depression and substance abuse.

DJ Nikki Hayes is another example of someone famous struggling with borderline personality disorder. Her struggles with inadequacy caused her to self-harm for decades. Currently, she shares her experiences through social media and a book she wrote, which discusses coping with this challenging condition. As she discusses in the book, being happy is a possibility with BPD. Each day is a learning opportunity regarding how best to manage this condition, as people are always in the process of improving.

The experience of living with BPD is unique to everyone. Those who live with this disorder should take the time needed to figure out what works best for them. Borderline personality disorder is a disrupting condition that makes it difficult to find joy in the simple things from everyday experiences. Therefore, focusing on feelings in the present and developing long-term habits that bring you peace is essential. Here are some tips on how to deal with the different situations you may encounter throughout the day.

Long-Term Vs. Present Moment

The key to creating the life you have always wanted is in balancing long-term changes with changes in the present. BPD can be overwhelming; small challenges become struggles. Other things, such as keeping a job or building a relationship, are also tricky.

Present Moment Coping Strategies

You may find that focusing on one feeling at a time helps whenever you feel overwhelmed. Below are some suggestions you may find helpful for the different feelings that might arise. It's okay if some things don't work for you. The key is to find whatever works for you to cope with each situation best for yourself. As you go along, you may probably develop your own tips to add to the list.

If You Are Feeling Angry, Frustrated, or Restless

In addition to affecting their lives, BPD sufferers feel on edge due to anger and frustration. Anger, in all its shades, is an unavoidable emotion that can sometimes feel overwhelming. In many cases, anger comes with thoughts about how things should be, how people should treat them, or the anger itself. A natural response to anger reactions is to focus on the person who caused them, which can result in significant conflicts.

Strategies to help navigate these situations:

- Breathe slowly

Try to take deep breaths and focus on each one for a moment. Exhale for longer than you inhale.

- Relax your body

You should focus on tightening and relaxing your muscles slowly if your body is tense. Focus on one muscle at a time.

- Try mindfulness techniques

You can calm your body and mind with mindfulness so you know when you are getting angry.

- Exercise

Exercise can help you work off your anger. Running is one of the best sports for releasing pent-up energy since it is a high-cardio sport. Or go for a brisk walk.

- Use up your energy safely in other ways.

Your angry feelings can be relieved in this way without hurting yourself or others. Try tearing up a newspaper, hitting a pillow, or smashing ice cubes in a sink.

- Do something to distract yourself mentally or physically

You can stop your anger from escalating by changing your situation, thoughts, or patterns. For example, you could try the following:

- Putting on upbeat music and dancing.

- Doing something with your hands, like fixing something or making something.

- Doing something creative like coloring or drawing.

- Writing in a journal.

- Taking a cold shower.

Violent or abusive outbursts can cause severe problems in your life and can damage relationships with those around you. You can use these simple techniques to cope with anger and frustration, but if you feel overwhelmed, you should consider getting help from a professional.

If You Want to Self-Harm

It can be hard to keep from harming yourself when you feel intense urges. However, there are steps you can take to help you make other choices:

1. Understand your patterns of self-harm

Identifying what triggers the urge to self-harm can help you recognize when the notion is coming. Reflecting on what happened after your self-harm is beneficial, even if you cannot resist the urge. When you have similar feelings in the future, you can understand them better.

You can break down your experience into the following categories:

2. Recognize triggers

Triggers are what give you the urge to hurt yourself. In addition to people, situations, anniversaries, and sensations, specific thoughts and feelings can also trigger self-harm behaviors.

Practice noting what was happening just before you self-harmed.

Did you have specific thoughts? Did a situation, person, or object remind you of something difficult?

3. Become aware of the urge to self-harm

Urges can include physical sensations such as racing heartbeats or feeling heavy, strong emotions such as sadness or anger, or a disconnection from yourself. It is also possible to have repetitive thoughts about harming yourself or how you might harm yourself.

You can reduce or stop self-harm by identifying your urges. Write down whenever you feel a sudden urge so you can recognize the situation quickly next time.

4. Identify distractions

It would be best if you distracted yourself to reduce the intensity of the desire to self-harm.

You can do this whenever you feel the urge or as soon as you realize you are about to hurt yourself.

Different distractions work for other people, and the same distraction may not work for you every time. How you distract yourself from anger feels very different from how you distract yourself from fear, so you must have a few strategies you can use.

Delaying self-harm.

You can also avoid self-harm by waiting five minutes before doing so. Initially, this may seem complicated, so do not worry if you find it difficult to wait that long. Consider increasing your waiting times between self-harms slowly and gradually.

If You Are Feeling Depressed, Sad, or Lonely

It is essential to distinguish sadness from depression since they are often confused. Clinically, depression refers to a cluster of symptoms, including feeling sad, while dysthymia refers to chronic depression lasting more than two years. Some of us may experience sadness daily. It is a feeling we all experience from time to time. Therefore, feeling sad is not the same as being depressed; it is simply a sign that a person is alive and has feelings.

Some simple things you can do to cope with feelings of sadness are:

- Wrap up in a blanket and watch your favorite TV show.

- Write all your negative emotions on a piece of paper and tear it up.

- Listen to a song or piece of music you find uplifting.

- Write a comforting letter to the part of yourself that is feeling sad or alone.

- Hug yourself or cuddle a pet.

We must learn to live with sadness, not get rid of it. Our goal should be to walk toward the things that matter to us despite negative feelings. You can do this by being there for yourself during difficult times instead of being hard on yourself. It is essential to recognize when you are lonely since it allows you to do something beneficial to embrace the situation without making things worse.

Contact a professional if you feel sad or lonely for a long time and these coping strategies do not work for you.

If You Are Feeling Anxious, Tense, or Panicky

The difference between fear, anxiety, and worry is that fear deals with the present, while anxiety/worry deals with the future. Anxiety problems are often accompanied by worry. Because of worry and anxiety, we usually get caught up in an endless cycle of *what-if* thoughts. While living with anxiety can be difficult, you can take measures that may help:

- Sit down with a hot beverage and drink it slowly, enjoying your senses as you smell and taste and notice the shape and weight of the mug.

- Breathe deeply ten times, counting each one aloud.

- Describe the room as accurately as possible, including the furniture, the color of the walls, the time, and the date. Tuning down the intense feelings can be achieved by focusing on the context.

- Bathe or shower in warm water. A soothing atmosphere combined with distracting physical sensations can help you change your mood.

If You Are Feeling Disconnected

When emotions come too quickly, too soon, and too much, it can be challenging to cope. People are more vulnerable to being at the mercy of emotions in the heat of the moment while hooked on intense emotions, which use excessive brain resources. To choose a behavior that aligns with personal objectives, you need to return to the moment and sit with a feeling without doing anything. When this occurs, "dropping the anchor" can be a helpful metaphor to remember how to proceed.

Imagine yourself as a boat at sea, being tossed around. You are experiencing rough weather, which represents all the external storms or crises around you that you cannot control. Rather than being tossed about by these rough seas, you drop the anchor. To steady your boat, you must steady yourself. By lowering your anchor, you will hold steady until the storm passes; the storm will still occur, but you will be less affected.

By dropping the anchor, you ground yourself in the moment of total emotional activity instead of drifting away. Here are ideas to help you drop the anchor:

- Chew a piece of ginger or chili.

- Clap your hands and notice the stinging sensation.

- Drink a glass of ice-cold water.

- Breath slowly.

- Listen to sounds around you.

- Walk barefoot.

- Wrap yourself in a blanket and feel it around you.

- Touch something rough or sniff something with a pungent smell.

Concentrate on the sensations that you are experiencing right now. Make sure you keep a box of different textures and scents (like perfume, a blanket, and smooth stones) handy.

Long-Term Ways to Cope

You probably understand by now that borderline personality disorder can affect how you perceive yourself, interact with other people, and respond to specific situations. Managing your emotions and actions is not easy, but that does not mean it is impossible.

To minimize the impact BPD has on your everyday life, it is crucial to learn how to self-manage. In the previous section, the discussion involved ways to cope with strong emotions that may arise and prevent you from making sound decisions. There are additional things you can do along with therapy that may help you control your BPD.

New coping skills can help you with the following:

- Developing your confidence in handling difficult situations.

- Maintaining a good level of functioning despite stressful conditions.

- Reducing your emotional distress.

- Preventing you from engaging in harmful behavior to escape emotional distress (self-harm, for example)

- Helping you to not engage in behavior that may destroy a relationship when you are upset (physical aggression, for example)

- Reducing the feeling of emotional dysregulation.

Thousands of coping skills exist to help you deal with stressful situations and the emotions that arise because of them. Some of these coping skills are as follows:

Educate Yourself

With borderline personality disorder, it is imperative to understand your condition. It has been shown clinically[15] that psychoeducational group (PEG) interventions reduce symptoms.

Education helps you:

- Identify your symptoms, so you can better understand them and how to manage them.

- Better understand how your therapist and doctor approach your treatment, allowing you to advocate for yourself.

- Recognize what may trigger angry outbursts or impulsive behavior.

Express Your Feelings

People with BPD can suffer from recurrent mood swings, anxiety, or irritability within a few hours of each other. Their anger and emptiness are often intense as well. That is why developing techniques for expressing these experiences are so important. You will be able to recognize unhealthy patterns of thoughts and make better choices. These may include:

- Journaling

- Drawing

- Painting

- Playing music

Mindfulness

Mindfulness is a process by which individuals are encouraged to be in the present moment. Rather than being absorbed in events of the past, future, or our own minds, it involves being present in what is happening right now. Mindfulness includes observing what is happening and feeling without judging, critiquing, or analyzing the situation.

Individuals can regulate emotions by developing emotional discipline and concentrating more on feelings. Anxiety and depression can also be calmed by mindfulness. It takes a lot of practice and conscious observation to cultivate mindfulness for many people. Meditation, for example, can help one achieve this state of mind. The good news is that mindfulness can ease the symptoms of people suffering from mental illnesses, including borderline personality disorder. Practicing mindfulness can be as simple as coloring with pencils or markers.

Many phone apps can remind you to meditate and provide you with appropriate exercises. You can try other forms of mindfulness if meditation does not work.

Distract Yourself

By improving your awareness of your mood, you will be able to identify early warning signs of changes in your attitude. You can distract yourself when you feel negative feelings begin to arise. Some ways to distract yourself include:

- Exercise.

- Watch a funny movie.

- Engage in a craft you enjoy, such as knitting or drawing.

- Listen to music. You might want to create a unique playlist that helps shift your mood.

- Do housework. Some people find cleaning an excellent way to manage their feelings.

- Take a bath or do something else you find relaxing.

Experiment until you find the best technique, depending on how you feel and where you are. If you are feeling down, you may discover wrapping yourself in a blanket and watching your favorite TV show can help. If you need to express feelings of anger, you may prefer to do something active or physical, like walking or running.

More Coping Skills

- Consider involving people close to you in your treatment to help them understand and help you.

- Seek treatment for related problems, such as substance misuse.

- Put limits on yourself and others. Learn how to express your emotions appropriately and in a way that does not alienate people or cause abandonment or instability.

- Reach out to other people with this disorder to share perspectives and experiences.

- Build a support system of people who can understand and respect you

- Maintain a healthy lifestyle, such as eating a healthy diet, staying active, and participating in social activities.

- Create your self-care kit (read below for some tips to do this).

- Do not blame yourself for the disorder but recognize your responsibility to treat yourself.

Your Self-Care Kit

A self-care kit is a collection of items that make you feel good, relieved, and relaxed.

When you build your self-care kit, you should customize it specifically to you, as every person's self-care experience will differ.

The following tips will help you put your box together:

- Find a box to put everything in as the first step.

- Diversify your self-care.

- Consider different time availability. Remember to add in some fast self-care ideas and some extended self-care ideas.

- Make self-care categories and include one item for each category in your self-care kit.

- Do not go overboard with the cost.

Most people can benefit from these self-care kit ideas:

Emotional Self-Care

- Journal

- Headphones

- Art supplies

- Tissues

- A list of friends or loved ones to call

Physical Self-Care

- Bath/Shower supplies

- Skincare

- Hair care

- Sleep care

- Favorite snacks

- Relaxing teas

- Good scents

Mental Self-Care

- Books

- Puzzles/Brain games

- Favorite movie or TV show

- Coloring book

- Journal

Social Self-Care

- List of your "people"

- Money for a social outing

- Compliments list

Practical Self-Care

- Budget planner

- Organization list

- Educational resources

- Vision board

Spiritual Self-Care

- Devotion/prayer book

- Crystals

- Manifestation list

- Relaxation/Meditation videos or music

- Positive affirmations

Healthier Coping Skills

Seeking treatment is one way to discover new coping skills. Dialectical behavior therapy (DBT) is one of many psychological treatments for borderline personality disorder that teaches patients healthier coping skills.

The next step is to shift the focus to those who love, live with, or work with someone with BPD. Most likely, they are at a loss about knowing what to do; this will be covered in the following chapters.

TAKEAWAYS

- As a result of borderline personality disorder, it isn't easy to find joy in everyday experiences. To achieve peace, it is crucial to focus on feelings that arise in the present moment and develop long-term habits.

- Present-moment coping strategies are based on the different feelings that might arise.

  ○ If you are feeling angry, frustrated, or restless

Breathe slowly, relax your body, try mindfulness techniques, exercise, use up your energy safely in other ways or do something to distract yourself mentally or physically.

- If you want to self-harm

Understand your patterns of self-harm, recognize triggers, become aware of the urge to self-harm, identify distractions, and delay self-harm.

- If you are feeling depressed, sad, or lonely

It is essential to distinguish sadness from depression since they are often confused. To cope with feelings of sadness, there are some simple steps you can take.

- If you are feeling anxious, panicky, or tense.

The difference between fear, anxiety, and worry is that fear deals with the present, while anxiety/worry deals with the future. While living with anxiety can be difficult, you can take measures that may help.

- If you are feeling dissociative or spaced out

You need to bring yourself back to the moment and sit with an emotion without acting. "Dropping the anchor" is a helpful metaphor when this occurs.

- Long-term ways to cope

Thousands of coping skills exist to help you deal with stressful situations and the emotions that arise because of them. Some that work for many people are listed below.

- Educate yourself

- Express your feelings

- Mindfulness

- Distract yourself

- Put together a self-care kit

Chapter Nine

A View from the Other End: Caring for Someone with BPD

As tricky as it is to portray mental illnesses and disorders in movies, *Silver Linings Playbook* (2012), a film directed by David O. Russell, illustrates borderline personality disorder well. In the movie, Pat (Bradley Cooper) and Tiffany (Jennifer Lawrence) suffer from BPD and bipolar disorder.

No one can deny that dealing with a loved one with a mental illness can be challenging. The story shows how their mental disorders affect their lives and families. A specific scene shows Pat angrily waking his parents because he cannot find his wedding video, which his parents have purposefully hidden from him because of how it makes him react. This results in him accidentally hurting his mother.

Similarly, Tiffany's parents are very concerned about Tiffany's handling of her disorder. Her family is appalled she is no longer ashamed to have multiple men seek her on the same day.

A movie such as *Silver Linings Playbook* may be dear to your heart because of how it acknowledges that mental illness is a part of society and overall has a positive outlook on it. As we can see in the movie, mental illnesses are more complex than they seem, and their impact is much broader than people can imagine. Thus, individuals around someone who has a mental illness should prioritize working on their own well-being first.

There is no doubt that BPD causes intense and stressful relationships because of the nature of its symptoms. Those with friends, family members, or loved ones who suffer from BPD understand the stress. When difficult situations arise, you may not know what to do or how to respond helpfully.

When a person with BPD is diagnosed, their family and friends are often left wondering what they can do to help them. It can be beneficial for a person with borderline personality disorder to have a support system around them that helps them manage their symptoms. You can use various strategies to help, which will be explained below.

Learn About Borderline Personality Disorder

Many misconceptions about BPD make it challenging to understand the condition. Living with someone with this disorder is often challenging, usually due to misunderstandings of the person's exacerbated attitude. Understanding the disorder, symptoms, and prognosis can help you better comprehend what your loved one is experiencing. To do this, always seek reliable resources, such as the National Institute on Mental Health (NIMH)[18]. You can also speak with a mental health care professional directly. Recognizing, accepting, and learning about borderline personality disorder will help supporters better understand the person with the condition and be able to relate to and communicate with them effectively.

Take Care of Yourself First

It is easy to get caught up in heroic efforts when trying to comfort and please someone you love with borderline personality disorder. When caring for someone with BPD, you may neglect your emotional needs in the process; however, this can lead to resentment, depression, burnout, and even physical illness.

Being run down and overwhelmed by stress makes it impossible for you to help others or enjoy sustainable, satisfying relationships. As in an in-flight emergency, you must put on your oxygen mask first to help those you love.

It is essential not to lose sight of your own needs and feelings when trying to provide support to a loved one with BPD. As they struggle to navigate the illness, many family members experience profound isolation, fear, and shame. Make sure you nourish your mind, body, and spirit by taking time for yourself. Get the assistance you need by engaging in individual therapy or joining a support group for loved ones of those with borderline personality disorder. Several great family programs are available that provide invaluable support and are designed specifically for people in your situation.

Validate Their Feelings

It is difficult for people without borderline personality disorder to understand the reactions and intensity of emotions experienced by others with the condition. It may be tempting to convince them otherwise or dismiss what they are feeling as irrational. It is essential to understand that those feelings are genuine to the person with the disorder. Therefore, it is both painful and counter-productive to dismiss their emotions.

When you validate, you accept and acknowledge what another person feels, regardless of whether you agree with their point of view or feelings. There is no need to agree with them to provide assurance. In other words, emotional validation is accepting and empathizing with another person. The following are some ways to validate emotional experiences:

Be Present

Emotional validation begins with being mindful whenever you share time with your loved one. You can do this by not staring at your phone and instead paying attention to what they say whenever you talk to them or by actively listening.

Listen and Reflect

Objective reflective listening involves summing up what the other person has said accurately. The goal is to learn and understand more deeply after active listening. Rather than saying, "There is no reason for you to feel this way," you can say, "I can tell you are hurting. It must be terrible to feel that way." Listen with empathy, compassion, respect, and unconditional positive regard.

Understand Other People's Reactions

Emotions can often take over the rational mind, causing us to lack concern for someone else's feelings. Understanding what the other might be thinking or feeling is crucial. Even though people cannot read minds, you can try to understand why the other person behaved in a certain way. It is essential to encourage another person to speak about their feelings by carefully choosing questions and expressions that let them know you understand how they feel.

A good example would be, "Did the comment I just made hurt your feelings?"

Understand the Situation

When interacting with someone, you must consider cultural and social context. In addition to reading the other's emotions, a situation can be enlightened if you account for contextual elements before formulating a hypothesis about their reaction. It is necessary to communicate this hypothesis to the other person so that they can confirm whether you are right.

For example, you might say to a person who a dog has previously bitten: "Are you comfortable with my dog near you?"

Normalize Emotions

A common belief is that people have "good" and "bad" feelings. Some emotions involve pain, so tagging them as "bad" is easier for us to understand, but all emotional reactions are normal. There is nothing wrong with feeling anxious, sad, or angry when you are going through a difficult situation. It is comforting to know that most people feel the same way in similar cases. For example, you could say, "I understand that you may be anxious or nervous. Speaking in front of the public can be difficult, especially the first time".

Have an Open Mind to the Emotional Experience of the Other

Having an open mind and accepting the other person's emotions will be beneficial to any interpersonal relationship. No matter what emotion another person is experiencing, it is their feeling— you must respect it. Every emotion has a meaning, so it is vital to make room for them all.

The importance of validation has become a central aspect of treatment for people with borderline personality disorder. You can help your relationship and your loved one by ensuring that your loved one feels heard and understood.

Set Boundaries and Stick to Them

While setting boundaries can be difficult when your loved one is suffering, the benefits of doing so cannot be overstated. Establishing and adhering to limits can give you both a sense of structure and peace. By encouraging your loved one to be accountable for their actions, you avoid having to tolerate unacceptable behavior; your relationship can ultimately be strengthened.

You should set boundaries in a way that is both helpful and realistic. Be calm and loving when introducing new ideas instead of accusing or shaming them. Initially, your loved one may perceive establishing boundaries as a sign of rejection. This is common among those that struggle with BPD because of their abandonment issues. Constant effort is required, but despite the hard times, limits can be incredibly beneficial to both of you.

Talk about boundaries when you and your loved one are calm rather than when you are arguing. Establish clear expectations about the behavior you will and will not tolerate from the person. For instance, you could say to your loved one, "If you cannot talk to me without insulting and screaming, I will leave the room."

You will want **TO DO** the following:

- Set limits in a calm and reassuring manner. Try telling them, "I love you, but I cannot handle the stress you cause me. This change is something I need you to do for me."

- Be sure all family members agree on boundaries and how to enforce them if they are violated.

- Think of setting boundaries as a process rather than introducing one or two limits simultaneously, rather than with a long list of them all at once.

You want **TO AVOID DOING** the following:

- You should not make threats and ultimatums that you cannot carry out. Your loved one will know the boundary is meaningless if you are not being consistent and fail to enforce the consequences mutually agreed upon.

- Never tolerate abusive behavior. Violence or verbal abuse should never be tolerated. The fact that your loved one has borderline personality disorder does not make their behavior any less real or any less damaging to you.

- Allow people with BPD to take responsibility for their actions; do not protect your loved one. You may need to leave them if they are unwilling to respect your boundaries and continue to make you feel unsafe. No matter how much you love them, always prioritize your self-care.

Enforce Emotional Boundaries

People who suffer from BPD experience emotions intensely. They may often want you to share the intensity of their feelings. They might try to create a circumstance that makes you angry as well.

The sooner you spot these trends, the sooner you break this co-dependent cycle. A great antidote to this behavior is being mindful of the other's feelings and validating them. The best thing you can do is tell them, "I see you are angry, and I understand why. I do not need to be angry to understand your anger. We can discuss this, but please do not yell at me or act abusively."

If they do not stop, you can tell them, "You are breaking a boundary we agreed to."

Be Consistent

Consistency is one of the most important aspects of dealing with someone with borderline personality disorder. The reason for this is that people with BPD test boundaries. Setting limits is a skill that takes time. You might find that your new limits are being pushed, stretched, or broken.

One cannot just change limits one day and expect adherence. Before things get better, they are likely to get worse. When you are consistent, they will test your boundaries less frequently.

Simplify Your Message

It is common for people with borderline personality disorder to distort what you say, confirming their worst suspicions about you or themselves. Even if the words are utterly unrelated to what you intended, a seemingly innocuous statement can quickly become a personal attack. This can obscure your true intentions, making communication impossible and damaging your ability to get through to your loved one. Remember that when you are talking with someone with BPD, especially on sensitive topics, emotions are likely so strong that both will be unable to think clearly.

Avoid misunderstandings at all costs. Keep your sentences short, simple, and direct. This will not rule out misinterpretation, but you can facilitate communication to minimize it as much as possible.

Encourage Responsibility

Responsibility means being accountable for the actions and obligations corresponding to the roles one plays in society.

In people with borderline personality disorder, responsibility is challenging to manage, as they oscillate between taking excessive responsibility or believing that others are responsible for their actions. In other words, it is hard for them to distinguish when something is their responsibility and when it is not.

When you see someone you love suffering, it can be hard to balance encouraging responsibility and caring for them. This does not mean letting them cope with their illness alone without support. However, try to resist the urge to save them from their mistakes.

Rather than jumping in to fix something they break while angry, let them figure it out for themselves. Do not bail them out if they get into credit card debt; the natural consequences of their actions can help them understand they need help. By stepping back, you can also cope more effectively without taking responsibility for things you have no control over. The experience can be profoundly empowering for both of you, even though it may seem counterintuitive initially.

Support Your Loved One's Treatment

It usually takes some time for people with borderline personality disorder to seek treatment. In many cases, they are reluctant to seek treatment because they believe their feelings are justified or previous negative experiences with mental health professionals have made them hesitant to try. However, professional mental health treatment is necessary to find peace and learn the required skills to cope with BPD symptoms. Making sure your loved one receives the support they need to make meaningful changes is an act of love, and you will probably be responsible for finding that treatment.

Some extreme cases will require residential mental health treatment programs to begin the healing process. To determine if medication and individual, group, or residential care is the best option for your loved one, consult a mental health professional.

Remember Your Role

A BPD diagnosis changes everything in someone's life, making everything revolve around the condition. In some cases, family and friends are unaware that this can be overwhelming. The person experiencing BPD symptoms has multiple options for discussing their situation and diagnosis, such as individual or group therapy. Maintaining a normal lifestyle at home is essential for them to feel understood and not left out.

Do not hide the problem from your family and friends. This will only lead to isolation and increased stigmatization. Keep your social life. Staying in touch with other family members and friends is essential to rejuvenate and relax and. Also, it is important that you can take a break and have someone else step in to take care of the person with BPD.

Finding time for light and neutral chats with your loved one is essential. Borderline personality disorder patients can benefit from light discussions because it encourages them to use their skills and express their interests. As a result, their sense of self and identity is strengthened. It is easy to forget to take time to discuss other life issues when dealing with conflicts and severe emotional concerns. During these light chats, try using humor and distraction to ease tensions. Make an agreement to avoid discussing more serious issues.

Know When You Need to Protect Yourself

Every relationship has needs, but supporting someone with BPD is more demanding than most. Knowing your limitations and recognizing when the relationship causes stress is essential. When you need a time-out, be self-aware and honest about it. Rather than seeing it as a rejection or criticism, consider it your self-care and part of a healthy relationship. When you can accept and care for yourself, you serve as a powerful role model for the person you are supporting.

When You Must Draw a Line

- Physical violence. It would be best if you did not tolerate the presence of physical violence in a relationship. It will result in someone getting hurt and the police getting involved—your safety is paramount.

- Having to avoid topics or interactions to keep the peace has a cost. You will be removing most of the potential communication, intimacy, and connection when too many topics or types of interactions need to be avoided.

- Change is not something your partner is willing to do. It is probably time to pack your bags if the person insists there is nothing wrong with them and that it is all your fault.

- You are consistently in a terrible mood. Is your life filled with misery all the time? You have got to take a step back from this relationship if you feel miserable every day.

Manage Crises

In the face of accusations and criticisms, it is essential that you listen and do not get defensive. Anger and heavy insults may be hurled at loved ones by people with borderline personality disorder in a rage.

Despite it being unfair, you must listen and possibly get emotionally hurt. Arguing what the other says implies that you think the other person's anger is unwarranted, leading to a tremendous crisis. It is important to remember that regarding BPD, anger usually indicates a desire to be heard, regardless of how distorted the feelings are. When you hear something you think might be true, admit it by saying, "I think I understand how you feel. I can see that I have hurt you, and I am sorry."

Always avoid telling people with borderline personality disorder how they should feel or behave. People with BPD are prone to rapid mood changes; anger can reverse quickly. As a result, anger may not be taken personally. Remind them that their feelings are valid and that you are there to support them through it.

Do Not Ignore Self-Harm Threats

BPD sufferers often threaten suicide or self-harm; many see these threats as manipulative and attention-seeking. People with borderline personality disorder are also more likely to commit suicide and harm themselves, so you should never ignore these threats.

Do not argue with your loved one if they threaten to take their own life or harm themselves. Never accuse them of manipulating you or just wanting attention. You should acknowledge that they are suffering and show your concern while maintaining your boundaries.

Even though you are never to blame if a loved one attempts suicide or self-harms, it is vital to do what you can to protect them. You should contact their doctor, **911**, or the **National Suicide Prevention Lifeline (1-800-273-TALK)** and stay with them until they are in the care of a professional. Make the person aware that you will act if you are concerned about their safety.

An Irreverent but Accurate Look at Mental Illness

A quick look back to the movie *Silver Linings Playbook* would be appropriate to picture the importance of relationships in mental health.

Throughout the film, Pat is both charismatic and terrifying, and when he meets Tiffany, a sultry and seriously depressed widow, he falls in love in an edgy and unpredictable way. With time, this bond turns into a healing one. Despite flaws and diagnoses, people still love, and loving others helps us work on ourselves.

There is no better way to describe the feeling of loving someone who has borderline personality disorder than the one portrayed in this movie. Some behaviors can make it hard to love the person, but the feeling is always there in the end.

The movie emphasizes the importance of mutual support for people. Managing symptoms and living up to one's potential can be achieved if mental illness is not feared.

While mental disorders are a reality and need to be treated with therapy or medication, the feelings and behaviors involved are not uncommon. Accepting loved ones with BPD and not being afraid or ashamed of them will be the key to creating a better life for everyone.

However, it is essential to recognize that dealing with someone with BPD can be challenging because you do not know exactly what to say, when, and how to say it. Other people sometimes describe the experience as walking on eggshells. Read on and learn what you should not do or say to a person with BPD to avoid making situations worse.

TAKEAWAYS

- The first step to helping someone with borderline personality disorder is understanding the condition, symptoms, and prognosis. Always seek reliable resources.

- Take care of yourself, consider your own needs and feelings, and get the assistance you need. Being run down and overwhelmed by stress makes it nearly impossible for you to help someone with BDP.

- Validate the feelings of those who have borderline personality disorder by being present, listening and reflecting, understanding other people's reactions, understanding the situation, normalizing emotions, and having an open mind to their emotional experiences.

- Set and reinforce healthy boundaries. Establish clear expectations about the behavior you will and will not tolerate from the person.

- Be consistent in maintaining your boundaries, knowing that others will try to discover ways to push or infringe on your limits.

- Simplify your message to avoid misunderstandings and encourage responsibility while resisting the urge to save them from their mistakes.

- Support their treatment by making sure they receive the support they need to make meaningful changes

- Maintaining a normal lifestyle at home is essential for them to feel understood and not left out.

- Protect yourself when there is physical violence or the number of boundaries is too high. Also, when change is not something your partner is willing to do or when you are consistently in a terrible mood.

- To manage crises, avoid telling people with borderline personality disorder how they should feel or behave.

- Pay attention if they threaten to take their own life or harm themselves; do what you can to protect them. Seek immediate help by calling 911. **National Suicide Prevention Lifeline (1-800-273-TALK)**

Chapter Ten
What to Avoid When Dealing with BPD

"My whole life, I've only known how to be like really good or really bad but being human is living in that kind of in-between space."

A TV show, *Crazy Ex-Girlfriend*, premiered in 2015, which is where the quote above originates. The show about Rebecca Bunch and her struggle with borderline personality disorder takes a refreshing and unique approach.

Mental health professionals and psychologists have consistently praised *Crazy Ex-Girlfriend* for accurately portraying mental health issues and personality disorders like BPD. In the show, Rebecca Bunch abandons her life and partnership at a top New York law firm after an accidental meeting with her former romantic interest. She longs to discover happiness, love, and adventure after experiencing chronic feelings of emptiness. Throughout the chapters, the show illustrates the reality of living with BPD and undergoing therapy, especially after you receive a formal diagnosis.

The show's portrayal of Rebecca Bunch as neither victim nor villain has received widespread praise. She is complicated, and that is okay. Each character has flaws and struggles, along with some beautiful aspects — this reflects humanity.

Another great message the show shares is that living with BPD does not mean you cannot function in society; your condition does not dictate your entire identity. Rebecca, for instance, performs well in school, gets along with her colleagues, and dresses appropriately for work. Since intimate relationships in her childhood led to pain, loss, fear, shame, and anxiety, she gets triggered by intimacy in relationships. Without triggers, Rebecca has no trouble going to work or maintaining friendships; however, those relationships can suffer when she is experiencing anxiety.

People with Borderline personality disorder have also praised the show. These people seemed impressed that the movie focused on the recovery process for those with mental health disorders. The movie did not emphasize the negative aspects of borderline personality disorder. Even if you are self-aware, coping with BPD is an endlessly challenging process, and the show captures this beautifully.

The show also perfectly portrays that there are no easy solutions. The pain of letting go and rebuilding is not hidden in brilliant musical scores.

As they navigate the ebbs and flows of their recovery, people with BPD long for what always seems out of reach...peace.

Crazy Ex-Girlfriend has educated the public about borderline personality disorder. The show spotlights the misconceptions about people with personality disorders. It shows how people with BPD manage their symptoms and go through the ups and downs of recovery and treatment.

There is nothing easy about living with someone who struggles with borderline personality disorder. Most of their symptoms might make you feel trapped unless the person receives treatment or you leave the relationship; however, you have more power than you realize. People with BPD can get better with the proper treatment, and their relationships can become more stable and rewarding with great support.

Living with someone who has borderline personality disorder can be difficult, mainly because they tend to overreact to situations. Despite this, you do not have to live with negativity. If you are living with someone who suffers from BPD, there are steps that you can take to ensure that your relationship remains healthy and stable. By enacting the following, you can improve your relationship with your partner, parent, child, sibling, friend, co-worker, or other loved one with BPD.

Tips on What to Avoid

When it comes to borderline personality disorder, knowing what to say is a challenge. Family, friends, and co-workers usually do not know when, how, and what to say to avoid conflicts or problems.

It is such a complex disorder that saying the wrong thing is common; you may feel like you are walking on eggshells. Additionally, it is easy to misunderstand the behaviors of individuals with BPD, which can result in miscommunication and frequent conflicts within relationships. Sometimes even therapists struggle to recognize clues when working with individuals with this diagnosis.

Conversely, people with borderline personality disorder feel like the language used to describe them is cold, detached, and uncaring; this only fuels their emotional sensitivity. Families and friends often fail to realize that people with BPD are highly vulnerable to conflict due to misdirected emotions, past experiences, and current stressors. Often, we observe them overreacting to a simple request or exploding when a minor inconvenience occurs. Many families worry about the emotional reactivity and risky reactions displayed by those with this disorder.

Supporting someone suffering from BPD will require acknowledging that boundaries must remain firm. The setting of limits can aid in the resolution of confrontations and arguments more quickly.

As you begin to set these boundaries, avoid the following:

Feeding into their need for attention

If you are close to someone struggling with BPD, you might observe that they constantly seek validation. They can do this by using different strategies, such as triangulation (i.e., bringing three or more people into an argument). It is essential not to fall into their trap repeatedly when it comes to a need for attention.

Validation is essential and healthy, but it becomes problematic when individuals seek assurance for doing things that are not okay. It means validating their difficult emotions and thoughts but not accepting their problematic coping strategies. BPD sufferers should be supported if they feel extreme anguish, but they should never be validated if they drink to feel better, for example.

Getting pulled into the "triangle" drama

Often, people with BPD misunderstand the intentions of loved ones when they are in a difficult situation, such as engaging in dangerous behaviors, because they feel bad about themselves. Though you may be trying to keep them safe, those with borderline personality disorder may interpret this as being unfairly treated and judged.

The individual with borderline personality disorder may talk to others instead of solving the problem with you. When this happens, those with BPD may go to a close family member to gossip, which leads them to want to participate in the argument; this is called triangulation. This strategy describes someone who involves more than two people in a chaotic situation, resulting in more chaos. This intervention, however, only worsens the situation.

When it comes to difficult situations involving people with BPD, avoid discussing the incident with others without connection to the original incident. In addition, if your loved one engages in this type of behavior, talk to them about how to stop it.

Feeling emotionally destroyed by impulsive remarks or behaviors

Relating to someone who suffers from borderline personality disorder is difficult, mainly because they may have problems managing anger and impulsiveness. If you feel entirely disrespected or devalued, express that to the person and create boundaries that make it clear that you will not tolerate abuse.

BPD sufferers can also be manipulative. Some of them are highly tuned into the other's emotions to decide how to "make their next move" to remain in control of the situation. If you find yourself in this position, remember that a stoic attitude and "downplaying" some of their attempts to get a reaction from you is more important than it seems. It is sometimes possible to change the entire encounter by having this response. If this method does not work, gradually distance yourself until your boundaries are re-established.

Becoming an emotional "prey"

It is common to hear individuals who have relationships with someone with BPD to express they feel like "prey." An example is a mother who feels her son uses her for money and then ignores her when he no longer needs her. Individuals with BPD who are not in treatment and possess sociopathic traits are prone to lacking empathy., Remember to make your boundaries clear, let the other person know what you need, and allow space between you as necessary.

Getting sucked into their "routine"

You can help your loved one with BPD by keeping routines and forming habitual behaviors. Nonetheless, allowing certain acts like late-night calls, visits to your house without notifying you, borrowing your items and not returning them, or driving your car for an extended time is not a good habit for people with BPD. And it is not healthy for you. You will have difficulty setting boundaries when you allow these behaviors to occur without being questioned.

Another characteristic of borderline personality disorder is the emotional chaos it brings. Explosions can occur cyclically, such as every spring, every school year, every anniversary, or every holiday. Whatever the case, you should avoid getting sucked into the person's cycle. You should not allow someone to gain control over you if the process is manipulative and intentional.

Deter, block, or switch things up to disrupt the cycle. A therapeutic approach is more appropriate if processes are unintentional; you will not be able to help someone if you are emotionally manipulated.

Always Being the "go-to" person

Many of us enjoy being the person everyone turns to when they need something done. Becoming the "go-to" person for individuals with borderline personality disorder may also mean that you are the one who is most manipulated and controlled. Eventually, the individual may believe you will always go the extra mile for them because they feel so close to you. Of course, additional efforts are always appreciated. Being needed is fine, but it is essential to set limits.

Allowing boundary crossings

Keeping solid boundaries may be necessary for you— no questions asked.

Doubts about boundaries can backfire in a relationship with someone with borderline personality disorder. If they push boundaries by manipulating or controlling you, it is up to you to stop them. This can be hard to achieve if you have never worked with firm boundaries.

Engaging in codependent behaviors

It is common for individuals with BPD to fear abandonment. As a result, unhealthy patterns of behavior may develop. When responding to these fears, be careful not to reinforce them. You can comfort or reassure those with BPD without enabling them.

Getting trapped in their fear can result in codependent behaviors. It can appear "sweet," "romantic," or even "charming" to others until time reveals the truth about how unhealthy it is. You can misinterpret it as closeness or support at first, but the individual may manipulate and control others when codependency develops in a family. An unhealthy combination of two individuals in a relationship results in them losing their own identities, values, beliefs, feelings, thoughts, etc.

Clarify the boundaries of the relationship if you feel "suffocated" or responsible for how they think. Those who suffer from borderline personality disorder often struggle with feelings of abandonment. They will do almost anything to reduce them. The conversation must be based on empathy, but empowering their codependency must be avoided at all costs.

Normalizing sexual promiscuity or risky behaviors

As discussed throughout previous chapters, some individuals with borderline personality disorder tend to push limits and engage in risky behaviors. Things will only get worse if risky and inappropriate behaviors are normalized. For example, someone with BPD may drink too much alcohol and have multiple unsafe intimate relationships while married. Therefore, do not normalize this behavior to make them feel better.

Believing they are capable of "snapping out of it"

Coping with the symptoms of BPD is not an easy task. Those with BPD cannot simply "snap out of it." Their behavior is altered by a combination of genetic, environmental, and social factors, personality, thought patterns, and learned behaviors. To help someone with BPD in the best possible way, try to understand why they behave as they do. Discover the causes and symptoms of the condition by reading and learning about it.

Normalizing things and minimizing your intuition

There is a good chance that something is seriously wrong if it appears to be so. Everyone gets angry sometimes, and we all experience intense emotions. And we will inevitably overreact at some point in our lives. Nevertheless, if these behaviors are persistent and severe, you need to address them. There can be no discounting its importance, and minimizing it doesn't help.

Setting clear boundaries is crucial in your relationship with someone with BPD. The condition makes it difficult for a person to manage their emotions. Living with BPD means dealing with self-image issues, mood swings, behavioral changes, insecurity, and instability.

People with BPD benefit from limits because they help organize their thoughts, comprehend the world, and relate to others in a healthy way. Your loved one will feel at peace amidst self-doubt, emotional chaos, and intense reactions whenever you show them what they should and shouldn't do.

Maintaining boundaries should always be your top priority, even when it seems impossible. When you feel exhausted, take a step back, work on your well-being, and then return. Your boundaries will pay off over time, and your relationship with the person you interact with will become healthy and caring.

Tips on what 'Not to Say'

You should avoid using these phrases with people with borderline personality disorder, as they can harm their mental and emotional health.

"You are emotionally unstable."

"You do not have to be angry all the time."
"You are overreacting."
"You were happy a few hours ago!"

People with BPD live in complex emotional worlds. Therefore, making assumptions about the other person's feelings and the reason for their reactions is invalidating. Despite the difficulty of understanding the emotional experience someone with BPD has, you should remain open-minded to the idea that how you experience life is different from theirs.

"Why can't you hold on to a relationship?"
"Why can't you consider the consequences before spending all your money?"

Those suffering from BPD require a lot of reassurance, resulting in more disagreements and arguments in their relationships, ultimately resulting in their inability to maintain a healthy relationship.

Moreover, someone with borderline personality disorder is not indifferent to the consequences of their actions; they simply think about them afterward.

"Do you think about self-harm? Have you tried it?"

You should avoid asking this kind of question at all costs because it can be triggering. For someone with BPD, this question can be extremely uncomfortable and challenging. Whenever someone tells you about their disorder, you should give them space and let them discuss their issues at their own pace. It is not okay to push them to satisfy your curiosity.

"Get your act together!"
"Try to be more positive."

The emotions of people with borderline personality disorder are openly displayed and exposed. Regardless if an emotion is good or bad, they feel it deeply. Many people mistake this as overreacting or not having everything together, but it is an honest expression of what someone with BPD is going through.

Positive feelings can be almost impossible to find when struggling with BPD, even on good days. A person with borderline personality disorder can be affected by genetics, the environment, or both, so telling them to be positive or get their act together may not be helpful.

"Stop being paranoid all the time."

"You are crazy."

"It is all in your head!"

"You are just seeking attention."

When it comes to mental health struggles, no one wants to hear any of these phrases. Be sensitive to your loved one's feelings and never invalidate them. Those with BPD are prone to guilt, anxiety, and self-doubt but are not crazy or selfish.

Your best course of action for helping your loved one with paranoia caused by borderline personality disorder is to reassure them and tell them you care about them.

"What caused your BPD?"

"Isn't Borderline personality disorder the same as bipolar disorder?"

"You do not have to tell others you have BPD."

"Isn't BPD impossible to recover from?"

"Everyone with BPD has a traumatic childhood."

There is an intense stigma when it comes to mental health diagnoses. For this reason, the stigma will grow by simplifying their condition or by avoiding speaking about the illness. These phrases are examples of what gives birth to stereotyping people with borderline personality disorder.

Not Saying Anything

When you have a loved one with borderline personality disorder, you know they will not go to bed without settling a dispute; even dismissing their concerns casually can be a significant problem for them.

Regarding what not to say to someone with BPD, not saying anything is also wrong. Alternatively, you can reassure them by telling them, "It is okay." You can also let them know that you will discuss it further at another time and that you understand how they feel, but you cannot meet their needs right now.

The experience of living with borderline personality disorder can be challenging for people with it as well as their families, friends, and romantic partners.

As you have seen previously, many people suffering from BPD must also deal with a burdening load of misunderstanding. Remember that these symptoms are uncontrollable, regardless of how upsetting they can be for you or others. BPD can sometimes seem like your loved one has turned into a completely different person when they are in the middle of an episode. Being kind to yourself and them is crucial, especially when they are having trouble coping with BPD.

Living with someone who has borderline personality disorder requires special care. People with BPD are not just a diagnosis; they are your family members, friends, and loved ones. Therefore, ensuring that your relationship with them is still positive and loving is essential. You must take care of yourself, especially since you can significantly impact their recovery and health.

The most important thing you can do for a person with BPD is to learn more about their disorder, identify the situations and behaviors that trigger intense reactions, and take steps to avoid them. It may be that they need to seek professional help as well. In fact, one of the best things you can do as a support person is to work with your loved one to find the best mental health treatment. While the symptoms of borderline personality disorder are hard to deal with and can leave family members feeling drained, disregarded, and frustrated, you must avoid responses that only add to the stress. Remember, with proper support and treatment, people with BPD can live healthier lives, and relationships can become more stable. Do your best to be patient and understanding if you are close to someone with BPD, but do not go beyond your limit. Incorporating some of these suggestions may help you have some peace and make you better about your decisions.

TAKEAWAYS

- Supporting someone with borderline personality disorder will require firm boundaries. The setting of limits can aid in the resolution of confrontations and arguments more quickly.

- Avoid feeding into their need for attention by not accepting their problematic coping strategies. Instead, focus on validating their difficult emotions and thoughts.

- Get out of the "triangle" drama, where you involve more people in a chaotic situation, creating more chaos.

- If you feel wholly disrespected or devalued, it is time to reiterate the established boundaries and make it clear that you will not tolerate abuse.

- Also, establish boundaries to avoid situations where they use you and then ignore you.

- Do not let the person manipulate you with their emotional chaos.

- Set limits so that you are not the only one that the individual with BPD can ask for help.

- Stop them when you see they are pushing boundaries by manipulating or controlling you.

- Avoid the codependency generated by the fear of abandonment of those who suffer from BPD.

- Do not normalize sexual promiscuity or risky behaviors.

- Try to understand why they behave as they do; this helps you accept that they cannot just "snap out of it."

- Never normalize things, nor minimize your intuition.

- Do not make assumptions about the other person's feelings and the reasons for their reactions.

- Avoid pushing them with complicated questions to satisfy your curiosity.

- Do not invalidate their feelings, tell them to be positive or get their act together.

Conclusion

Borderline personality disorder is one of the most misunderstood and stigmatized mental health conditions. It has been called "one of the great psychiatric disorders" since it affects every aspect of a person's life; however, it is not accurately understood by non-sufferers. You are probably familiar with the fact that BPD is a diagnosis that millions of people suffer from, that fighting through your symptoms will only cause more emotional pain, that help is available, and that you are never entirely alone in your experience.

BPD is a complex condition for anyone to live with, but if you know what you are dealing with, it does get easier. Hopefully, this book helped to shed light on BPD and helped you make sense of it. The management of borderline personality disorder is a lifelong, intensive process. It requires an exceptional level of self-awareness and commitment to your well-being. After becoming familiar with your own emotions and behaviors, you can learn healthy adjustment mechanisms to overcome obstacles.

People with BPD face significant challenges that vary depending on multiple factors, such as their environment and history. BPD sufferers share some of the same characteristics, but their experiences are unique. For instance, those who live with BPD may share the experience of emotional sensitivity, but how each experience will differ. It is possible for some people to feel threatened by coworkers who are doing better than them, while others might feel fearful of being abandoned.

Patients with BPD tend to feel too much and act too quickly. Because of their predisposition for emotional sensitivity, getting caught up in the emotion of the moment, and all the behaviors they do to manage their emotional rollercoaster, they develop patterns of complex responses that can be hard to understand for those around them.

Borderline personality disorder is a serious, chronic mental illness that requires lifelong care and coping skills; both the individual and their loved ones will encounter difficulties in different aspects of their lives. Everyone with this condition needs to recognize their weaknesses and understand how they can overcome them. Most importantly, those diagnosed with borderline personality disorder need to seek emotional support from family, friends, and trusted healthcare professionals.

If you are close to someone diagnosed with BPD, remember to put yourself in their shoes and let go of your assumptions. Their lives are complicated because they are extremely sensitive in every situation and cannot comprehend their own feelings, typically leading to problematic behaviors. Their erratic emotions and interpretations make it difficult for them to succeed in projects. In addition, relationships are challenging as they feel threatened most of the time; social strategies often do not work.

If you are close to someone with BPD, it is crucial to recognize that they are suffering; the destructive and hurtful behaviors are a response to deep emotional pain.

You can get caught up easily in heroic attempts to appease someone with BPD. You may put most of your energy into the person with borderline personality disorder at the expense of your own emotional needs. When you are run down and overwhelmed by stress, you cannot help others or enjoy sustainable, satisfying relationships; therefore, taking care of yourself is the first step in caring for someone with BPD.

While there is no magic cure for BPD, with the proper treatment and support, many people can get better and enjoy more satisfying relationships. Additionally, listening to your loved one and acknowledging their feelings are excellent ways to help someone with BPD. By managing your reactions, establishing firm boundaries, and improving communication, you can improve your relationship with them. The information in this book will not solve your relationship problems automatically, but it will help you understand your situation and deal with difficulties constructively.

Borderline personality disorder is a lifelong mental disorder. Fortunately, the mental health of BPD sufferers is something they can improve to a great extent if they begin making changes immediately. Hopefully, this book provided information on better understanding the nature of borderline personality disorder.

If you have BPD, the most effective way to understand this condition is to work with a trained therapist who can help you further address your personal experiences with the disorder. With the proper support, you can put these strategies into practice, enabling you to control your emotions better, reduce isolating behaviors and punish self-destructive thoughts to achieve a great life. However, please remember that this book is a surface-level overview of the disorder.

Millions of people worldwide with BPD have found the proper treatment and are now at peace with who they are. It is also important not to underestimate the power of making simple changes in your daily life to help you manage your symptoms, such as taking care of your body or practicing meditation.

BPD may seem like a daunting condition, but with the proper knowledge and support, you can lead a successful life just like anyone else. Learn more about your BPD and seek professional help if needed. Be aware of your triggers while also being mindful of how you feel.

Now that you know more about BPD, it is time you try to tackle it head-on. You cannot just let it get the best of you, especially when there are so many ways to manage your condition effectively. Knowing how to manage BPD is a lot, but specific points will make everything much more manageable. With these strategies, you will be able to deal with this disorder effectively. There will still be some hurdles along the way, but hopefully, these references have clarified and made things easier for you.

Borderline personality disorder is a condition that needs to be discussed openly; the more information, the better. The disorder affects many people yet is poorly understood, making resources for people with BPD and those close to them more valuable.

Ultimately, borderline personality disorder is a mental condition that should be treated. It is time to stop considering BPD as a character flaw rather than a common but treatable mental condition. Knowledge is power, and awareness of your disorder can help improve your life. I hope you found the information in this book to be beneficial. Take advantage of what you learned. Do not delay taking the necessary steps to help yourself or someone with BPD.

If you found this book helpful, please take a moment to leave a positive review.

It can help someone living with BPD, either the one with the condition or someone in a personal or work relationship with the sufferer. It will only take a couple of minutes and it can make a difference in the many lives of people experiencing borderline personality disorder. *Thank you.*

amazon.com   https://bit.ly/4beN0OO

amazon.uk   https://amzn.to/3xk8ig1

amazon.ca   https://amzn.to/3Wc985o

amazon.au   https://amzn.to/3FGWmVD

Are You Interested in a Couple of <u>FREE BONUSES</u>?

Click HERE or SCAN the Code below to get your ***FREE PDF copy Now***!

Scan me

Chapter Eleven
REFERENCES

1.	Doctor in psychology, professor, researcher, author; American Marsha Linehan created a theoretical model of treatment for patients with borderline personality disorder (BPD). Today, she is an international reference in suicide prevention.

2.	https://www.theravive.com/therapedia/borderline-personality-disorder-dsm--5-301.83-(f60.3)

3.	Chapman J, Jamil RT, Fleisher C. Borderline Personality Disorder. [Updated 2022 May 2]. In: StatPearls [Internet]. Treasure Island (FL): StatPearls Publishing; 2022 Jan-. Available from: https://www.ncbi.nlm.nih.gov/books/NBK430883/

4.	Barber, T. A., Ringwald, W. R., Wright, A. G. C., & Manuck, S. B. (2020). Borderline personality disorder traits associate with midlife cardiometabolic risk. *Personality Disorders: Theory, Research, and Treatment,* *11*(2), 151–156. https://doi.org/10.1037/per0000373

5.	Levy, J. (2018, April 29) *Borderline Personality Disorder: 4 Natural Ways to Help BPD Treatment.* Dr. Axe Recovered from: https://draxe.com/health/borderline-personality-disorder/#Ways_to_Help_Borderline_Personality_Disorder_Treatment

6.	Frydl, A (2019, May 9) Running as therapy: Dr. Deborah Parker shows how exercise is critical for managing borderline personality disorder. Nueva Scotia Health. Recovered from: https://www.nshealth.ca/news/running-therapy-dr-deborah-park er-shows-how-exercise-critical-managing-borderline-personality

7.   Salters-Pedneault, Kristalyn. "Being Married to a Person With Borderline Personality Disorder." Verywell Mind, www.verywellmind.co m, 12 July 2020, https://www.verywellmind.com/borderline-personalit y-and-marriage-425222.

8.   Smith M, South S. Romantic attachment style and borderline personality pathology: A meta-analysis. Clin Psychol Rev. 2020;75:101781. doi:10.1016/j.cpr.2019.101781

9.   Miano A, Dziobek I, Roepke S. Characterizing couple dysfunction in borderline personality disorder. Journal of Personality Disorders. 2018;34(2):181-198. doi:10.1521/pedi_2018_32_388

10. Sansone RA, Sansone LA. Sexual behavior in borderline personality: A review. Innov Clin Neurosci. 2011;8(2):14-8.

11.   De Genna NM, Feske U, Larkby C, Angiolieri T, Gold MA. Pregnancies, abortions, and births among women with and without borderline personality disorder. Women's Health Issues. 2012;22(4):e371-7. doi:10.1016/j.whi.2012.05.002

12. Ona, P. E. Z. (2020). Acceptance and Commitment Therapy for Borderline Personality Disorder: A Flexible Treatment Plan for Clients with Emotion Dysregulation. New Harbinger Publications

13. Juurlink, T. T., Vukadin, M., Stringer, B., Westerman, M. J., Lamers, F., Anema, J. R., ... & Van Marle, H. J. (2019). Barriers and facilitators to employment in borderline personality disorder: A qualitative study among patients, mental health practitioners and insurance physicians. PLoS One, 14(7), e0220233.

14. Elliott, B., & Konet, R. J. (2014). The connections place: A job preparedness program for individuals with borderline personality disorder. Community mental health journal, 50(1), 41-45.

15. Ridolfi, M. E., Rossi, R., Occhialini, G., & Gunderson, J. G. (2019). A Clinical Trial of a Psychoeducation Group Intervention for Patients With Borderline Personality Disorder. The Journal of clinical psychiatry, 81(1), 19m12753. https://doi.org/10.4088/JCP.19m12753

16. https://frtc.ltd/blog/biosocial-theory-bpd

17. https://philosiblog.com/2013/10/02/a-clever-person-solves-a-problem-a-wise-person-avoids-it/

18. https://www.nimh.nih.gov/

National Suicide Prevention Lifeline (1-800-273-TALK)

Printed in Great Britain
by Amazon

46545699R00096